THIS CIVILISATION IS FINISHED
Conversations on the end of Empire—and what lies beyond

Rupert Read and Samuel Alexander

THIS CIVILISATION IS FINISHED:
Conversations on the end of Empire—and what lies beyond

Published by the Simplicity Institute, Melbourne 2019

www.simplicityinstitute.org

Copyright © 2019 Rupert Read and Samuel Alexander

Cover image by Jerzy Gluszek © 2019

Cover design by Sharon France © 2019

Layout and typesetting by Sharon France (Looking Glass Press)

Typeset by in Trajan and Stone Sans

ISBN: 978-0-9942828-3-5 (paperback)

'A brave and necessary conversation, which digs deep into ideas which will make many people—including many greens—uncomfortable. This book should help everyone to question their own assumptions.'
   —Paul Kingsnorth, co-founder of The Dark Mountain Project

'Decades of pretence are coming to a close. Rapid changes in our climate are waking us up to the reality that we and the Earth are one system. The wasted decades mean we are woefully unprepared for the consequences of our actions. Read and Alexander show that our civilisation of separation is finished. They invite us to start having difficult but creative conversations about the shape of whats to come and how we might get there. A helpful balm for climate anxiety—this book leaves you feeling that something could be salvaged and something better might even be born.'
   —Jem Bendell, author of 'Deep Adaptation'

'Far from urging dejection or despair, these authors look at the greatest challenges facing humanity with unusual honesty—and yet they find meaning, purpose, and perhaps even hope in unexpected places.'
   —Richard Heinberg, author of *The End of Growth*

'Bring your fear, your despair and your hope to this book—it will nurture them all with sharp and nuanced insight.'
   —Kate Raworth, author of *Doughnut Economics*

'We are facing collapse on multiple levels, but the good news is that the crises we face are interconnected—they share a root cause, and there is a systemic strategy for beginning to solve them simultaneously. This book is an example of the kind of 'big picture activism' we need in order to get people to zoom out, see their commonalities with unlikely allies, and unite voices for a fundamental shift in direction. We have the opportunity to create a people's movement; a coalition like never before. I agree with Rupert and Samuel that the end of civilisation as we know it gives us an opportunity to create the conditions for both human and ecological wellbeing. They are among the rare academics who have the courage to go beyond the confines of narrow specialisation to speak out, to question the dominant narrative.'

—**Helena Norberg-Hodge, author of** *Ancient Futures*

CONTENTS

Acknowledgements

Deep thanks to Peter Kramer, Victor Anderson, and Aseem Shrivastava for illuminating readings of the manuscript. Thanks also to Kanada Gorla for insightful conversation on the concept of 'civilisation', and to Cathy Rowett for ideas concerning what humanity's great achievements really are. Furthermore, we are extremely grateful to our editor, Antoinette Wilson, for her meticulous reading of our manuscript, and to Sharon France, for her timely and stylish work typesetting the book and designing the cover. The cover image was kindly provided by Jerzy Gluszek (http://www.gluszek.com/).

There is an abyss opening up before us. It challenges everything we thought we knew about our culture and about nature. We need to look into it and concentrate on what we can see.

—Paul Kingsnorth

1. GAZING INTO THE ABYSS

Samuel Alexander (SA): Rupert, I would like to invite you into a space of uncompromised honesty. Let us engage each other in conversation, not primarily as scholars wanting to defend a theory, or as politicians seeking to win votes or advance a public policy agenda, or even as activists fighting for a cause, but instead, just as human beings trying to understand, as clearly as possible, our situation and condition at this turbulent moment in history.

When I look at the world today, I see the vast majority of academics, scientists, activists, and politicians 'self-censoring' their own work and ideas, in order to share views that are socially, politically, or even personally palatable. There are times, of course—often there are times—when we must be pragmatic in our modes of communication, and shape the expression of our ideas in ways that are psychologically digestible, compassionate, or even crafted to be attractive to an intended audience. But the more we do that, the more constrained we are from saying what we really think; the less able we are to look unflinchingly at the state of things and describe what we see, no matter what we find. If we never find ourselves in spaces of unconstrained openness, we might not even know what we really think, hiding truths even from ourselves.

It seems to me that one of the first principles of intellectual integrity is not to hide from truths, however ugly or challenging they may be. Yet there are truths today which I feel many people are choosing to ignore, not because they do not see them or understand them, but because they *do not want* to see or understand them. Truth, as any philosopher knows, is a contested term. But perhaps in what is increasingly called a 'post-truth' age, time is ripe to reclaim this nebulous notion, to try to pin it down, not in theory but in practice. That is to say, I am inviting you, Rupert, to practise truthfulness with me, to share thoughts on what we *really think*, and to do so, as far as possible, without filtering our perspectives to make them appear anything other than what they are. This may require some bravery, of course, because if thou gaze long into an abyss, as Nietzsche once said, the abyss may also gaze into thee. Have we the courage? Will our readers have the courage to stay with us on this perilous and uncertain journey?

My invitation to you is not, of course, arbitrary. It seems to me that you are amongst a very small group of thinkers today who have already started the process of speaking 'without filters'. I've seen you deliver lectures to your students saying things that most academics would not dare even to think, let alone say out loud in public. I've read articles of yours that manifest the uncompromised honesty that I hope will inform, perhaps even inspire, this dialogue. One of the articles to which I refer, and which now entitles this book, is called 'This Civilisation is Finished.'[1] Let that bold and unsettling statement initiate our conversation. No doubt it will require some unpacking. What did you mean when you declared that this civilisation is finished?

Rupert Read (RR): Thanks Sam. It is a privilege, in at least two ways, to be able to conduct this dialogue with you. First, it's a privilege to be in dialogue on this vital matter with *you*, whose work on degrowth and voluntary simplicity is, in my opinion, simply the best there is. But I also mean that it's a privilege, a wonderful luxury, to be able to have this conversation at all, because it is quite possible that in a generation's time, or possibly much less than that even, such conversations will be an unaffordable luxury.

It is quite possible that, although we are living at a time that is already nightmarish for many humans in many ways (let alone for non-human animals), we will come to look back on these times, if we are alive to look back on them at all, as extraordinarily privileged. Right now people such as you and me don't have to spend much of our time scrabbling for food and water or looking over our shoulders worrying about being killed. So we have a responsibility to make the most of this privilege.

What I've just expressed will strike some readers as exaggerated for effect. It is not. It is simply an attempt to level with everyone; to take up your invitation, Sam, and join you in a space of uncompromised honesty. Environmentalists are often accused of being doom-mongers. I think that the accusation is largely false, because I think that almost all environmentalists incline in fact to a Pollyanna-ish stance of undue optimism. This might prompt an accusation of me being a fear-monger or alarmist. I'm not an alarmist. I'm *raising the alarm*. When there's a fire raging—as is the case right now, as I write, across the UK and across the world including in forests that are our planetary lungs—then that's what one needs to do. Raise the alarm. This elementary distinction—between being an alarmist and justifiably raising the alarm—is exactly the distinction that Winston Churchill drew, under similarly challenging (though actually *less* dangerous) conditions, in the 1930s.

If people are feeling paralysed right now, I think it is probably because they are stuck between false hopes. On the one hand, there is the delusive lure of optimism, the hope that there will be a techno-fix that will defuse the climate emergency while life more or less goes on as usual. This is, I believe, in a desperately-dangerous way keeping us from facing up to climate reality. On the other hand, there are dark fears that people mostly don't voice and don't confront. My message, far from being paralysing, is liberating. One is liberated from the illusory comfort—that deep down most of us already know is illusory—of eco-complacency. One is able at last to look one's fears full in the face. One is able at last to see the things that the other half didn't want to see. And then to be freer of constraint in how one acts.

One of the ideas in the work of philosopher Ludwig Wittgenstein that most deeply inspires me is that the really difficult problems in philosophy have nothing to do with cleverness or intellectual dexterity. What's really difficult, rather, is to be *willing* to see or understand what one doesn't want to. After years of denial, and years of desperate hope, I finally reached a point where it was no longer possible for me to not see and understand the fatality that is almost surely upon us.

I have come to the conclusion in the last few years that this civilisation is going down. It will not last. It cannot, because it shows almost no sign of taking the extreme climate crisis—let alone the broader ecological crisis—for what it is: a long global emergency, an existential threat. This industrial-growthist civilisation will not achieve the Paris climate accord goals;[2] and that means that we will most likely see 3–4 degrees of global over-heat at a minimum, and *that* is not compatible with civilisation as we know it.

The stakes of course are very, very high, because the climate crisis puts the whole of what we know as civilisation at risk. By 'this civilisation' I mean the hegemonic civilisation of globalised capitalism— sometimes called 'Empire'—which today governs the vast majority of human life on Earth. Only some indigenous civilisations/societies and some peasant cultures lie outside it (although every day the integration deepens and expands). Even those societies and cultures may well be dragged down by Empire, as it fails, if it fells the very global ecosystem that is mother to us all. What I am saying, then, is that this civilisation *will* be transformed.[3] As I see things, there are three broad possible futures that lie ahead:

(1) This civilisation could collapse utterly and terminally, as a result of climatic instability (leading for instance to catastrophic food shortages as a probable mechanism of collapse), or possibly sooner than that, through nuclear war, pandemic, or financial collapse leading to mass civil breakdown. Any of these are likely to be precipitated in part by ecological/climate instability, as Darfur and Syria were. Or

(2) This civilisation (we) will manage to seed a future successor-civilisation(s), as this one collapses. Or

(3) This civilisation will somehow manage to transform itself deliberately, radically and rapidly, in an unprecedented manner, in time to avert collapse.[4]

The third option is by far the least likely, though the most desirable, simply because either of the other options will involve vast suffering and death on an unprecedented scale. In the case of (1), we are talking the extinction or near-extinction of humanity. In the case of (2) we are talking at minimum multiple megadeaths.

The second option is very difficult to envisage clearly, but is, I now believe, very likely. One of the reasons I have wanted to have this dialogue with you, Sam, is so that we can talk about how we can prepare the way for it. I think that there has been criminally little of that, to date. Virtually everyone in the broader environmental movement has been fixated on the third option, unwilling to consider anything less. I feel strongly now that that stance is no longer viable. And, encouragingly, I am not quite alone in that belief.[5]

The first option might soon be as likely as the second. It leaves little to talk about.[6]

Any of these three options will involve a transformation of such extreme magnitude that what emerges will no longer in any meaningful sense be *this* civilisation: the change will be the kind of extreme conceptual and existential magnitude that Thomas Kuhn, the philosopher of 'paradigm-shifts', calls 'revolutionary'. Thus, one way or another, *this* civilisation is finished. It may well run in the air, suspended over the edge of a cliff, for a while longer. But it will then either crash to complete chaos and catastrophe (Option 1); or seed something radically different from itself from within its dying body (Option 2); or somehow get back to safety on the cliff-edge (Option 3). Managing to do *that* miraculous thing would involve such extraordinary and utterly unprecedented change, that what came back to safety would still *no longer in any meaningful sense be* this civilisation.[7]

That, in short, is what I mean by saying that this civilisation is finished.

2. CLIMATE CHAOS:
BLACK SWAN OR WHITE SWAN?

SA: The notion of a 'black swan' event was introduced into the cultural lexicon by Nassim Taleb to signify a radically unexpected and improbable event that has profound consequences. Something that would lead to the end of civilisation as we know it would presumably be unexpected—a black swan—because otherwise people would have done something about it. Presumably. Yet you call dangerous anthropogenic climate change a 'white swan'. What are you getting at?

RR: Much of my work in recent years concerns the impact of improbable events that can be 'determinative', wiping out the effects of decades of normality or 'progress'. For instance, there is my work alongside Nassim Taleb, arguing this case *vis-à-vis* genetic modification;[8] that is, we argue that there is a strong precautionary case against GMOs (even if there is not a strong 'evidence-based' case against them), because there is a risk of *ruin* implicit in genetic engineering, if it goes wrong.

But there is a basic way in which the case of climate is very different from the case of GMOs. For it has been shown beyond reasonable doubt that anything remotely like a business-as-usual path puts us on course for climate Armageddon.[9] The basic science of climate change is as compelling as that of tobacco causing cancer,[10] and so we cannot pretend that we do not *know* that it would be insanity to carry on down the road we are driving.

Ever-worsening man-made climate change (ever-worsening, that is, barring a system change, a radical and swift transformation in our attitude to our living planet) is therefore *not* properly a potential 'black swan' event. It's a *white* swan: an expected event. It is, quite simply, what anyone with a basic understanding of the situation should now expect. And this means that, tragically, the default expectation, barring us doing something extraordinary, must be for our future to look like (1) or at best (2) from the list I just outlined.

True, there are some significant grey-flecked feathers in the white plumage. We don't know the exact 'climate-sensitivity' of the Earth system,[11] and we don't know all the feedbacks that are likely to kick in, nor just how bad most of them will be. We don't know how long we've got.

Crucially, these uncertainties, properly understood, *underscore* the case for radical precautious action on preserving our livable climate,[12] for uncertainty cuts both ways. It might end up meaning that the fearful problem one was worried about turns out to be somewhat more tractable than we'd feared. *Or* it might end up meaning that it turns out even worse than expected.

There is an asymmetry here, for as the worst-case scenario for something potentially ruinous gets worse, we need ever more strongly to guard against it. The possibility of a relatively tractable or even beneficial scenario (as with the possibility that anthropogenic climate change may make it feasible for the world's best champagne to be produced in Britain) is always outweighed by the possibility of a yet more catastrophic scenario (as with the remote but non-zero possibility that if temperatures keep rising, we induce a runaway feedback—perhaps via massive methane releases—and we end up with the extinction of virtually all life on Earth). An infinitely bad possible downside cannot be outweighed by a possible upside, however good.

So, even the grey feathers among the swan's plumage change the situation not one bit—except to underline how we not only face a potential catastrophe but furthermore one that may exceed most of our models.[13] It is beyond reasonable doubt that we are at present driving ourselves toward a cliff, maybe one with a fatally larger drop below it than our best current science suggests. We desperately need to slow down. But we show little sign of doing so.

Catastrophic climate change is a white swan, and even the odd grey or black feather only underscores how badly we are exposed to it—to catastrophe.[14] We are, that is, in a long emergency, quite possibly a permanent emergency. Only it doesn't feel that way most of the time, because the white swan isn't yet flapping right in front of our eyes—though the increasingly chaotic weather frequently gripping us is a series of dramatic wake-up calls, wake-up calls that finally, thankfully, seem to be starting to wake an increasing number of us up.

So we are all, in effect, to some degree in climate-denial. We seem blinded by the light that this civilisation compulsively gives off. I guess that's why you and I are having this conversation. To see if it's yet possible to lift the blinders. And to assess what we can still hope and work for, assuming we don't succeed in bringing off an unprecedented civilisational transformation.

3. TECHNOLOGICAL SEDUCTIONS

SA: I feel that one of the main reasons people are blind to the dire situation you describe is because of a deep-seated faith in technology. I call this faith 'techno-optimism', which can be broadly defined as the belief that science and technology will be able to solve the major social and environmental problems of our times without fundamentally re-thinking the structure or goals of our growth-based economies or the nature of Western-style, affluent lifestyles.

What is so seductive about this 'techno-fix' approach is that it is politically, economically, and socially palatable. It provides govern-ments, businesses, and individuals with a means of responding to environmental problems (or being seen to respond to environmental problems) without actually confronting the underlying systemic and cultural issues that are driving the crises. Don't worry, is the message, technology will save us from ourselves. It is all very non-confronting. Too good to be true, one might say.

RR: Exactly so. Techno-optimism sends us to sleep, as it de-politicises and de-moralises crisis. It encourages us to believe that everything comes to us in the forms of problems (rather than tragedies or myster-ies); that there are no insoluble problems; and that radical politics and ethics can take a permanent backseat to the magic of the techno-in-dustrial complex.

I think that techno-optimism is partly rooted in technophilia: the love of technology. That might sound like a harmless (or even posi-tive) thing, but it isn't, if it is an irrational love (as, increasingly, one strongly suspects it is), or if it replaces love of people or of nature.

The ultimate root of both technophilia and techno-optimism is in humanism. Many of us have been taught to assume that humanism is obviously good, the only viable alternative to religious superstition. But there are a number of reasons why humanism is not good. Let me illustrate them:

If humanism puts an end to all religion and spirituality, then that may be throwing the baby of attitudes of reverence and sacredness out with the bathwater of the Old Testament God. And we then risk taking a huge step into a brave new unknown world, a world which in effect has only people in it.[15]

Furthermore, we should ask (of humanism): human as opposed to what? If the answer is *as opposed to non-human animals/to nature*, then we can unmask humanism; unmask it as simply an unwarranted attitude of superiority to the rest of creation. As if, having ditched gods, we were to declare ourselves gods.[16]

None of this should actually be surprising, because what does humanism, as an alternative to the old religions, really amount to? The worship, not of God, but of ourselves. And, pretty obviously, given our record, it just isn't remotely clear that we deserve to be worshipped. We should give up such a hubristic over-estimate of our own abilities and wisdom. It is past time we took up a humbler (more precautious) attitude[17] to our place in the natural order.[18]

We need, of course, to take advantage of appropriate technologies: 'passive solar' being a wonderful example, a way of changing housing in colder climes such that houses are heated without the need to burn anything.[19] But we badly need to escape the delusion of techno-optimism. We need to understand that many of the profound challenges ahead will only be faced up to if we are willing to change our way of life, the way we organise ourselves and, yes, our values. Humanism keeps stoking techno-optimism and technophilia because, since we love and have entire confidence in what are widely assumed to be our greatest products—technologies—we tacitly find glory in ourselves.

Loving technology is merely loving ourselves by proxy.

Actually, I don't believe that technologies *are* our greatest 'products'. I think that that laurel ought to go to our finest systems of valuation: to morality, to philosophy, to great art. Technology ought to be our servant, while ethics and these most profound emanations of our collective and individual imaginations ought to be our masters.

Last but not least: technophilic assumptions are plain reckless at a time of likely civilisational failure, because it is possible that relatively few technologies will survive such a failure; and, as they flicker out, they may plunge us into yet worse travail. Let's come back to this point.

So: most humanism nowadays stokes an unwarranted and reckless techno-optimism. I want to redeem those aspects of humanism (such as philosophy and art at their best) which do not. But the best context for that is to stop pretending that we are not animals, to stop misleadingly separating ourselves from nature, to jettison the arrogance of 'anthropocentrism'. It's time to leave behind the label of humanism.[20]

4. GEO-ENGINEERING AND THE PRECAUTIONARY PRINCIPLE

SA: I worry that the more that technological solutions fail humanity, the more we will look to technology to solve the same (now worsening) problems. But isn't this the definition of idiocy? That is, looking for something in the same place you didn't find it last time you looked; or trying the same thing that didn't work last time and expecting a different result. A particularly alarming example is geo-engineering. I'm not talking here about planting lots of trees—which can be understood to be a form of geo-engineering (aka 'climate-engineering'), and one I'd support. I'm talking about things like spraying sulfate aerosols into the stratosphere in the hope of creating a global cooling effect to counteract the warming effect from burning fossil fuels. The more developed the climate crisis becomes, the more attractive geo-engineering experiments like this might seem. But this could well be mistaking the poison for the cure. You mentioned the Precautionary Principle earlier. How do you see that principle applying to geo-engineering?

RR: First, I'd query whether, if done in the right way, tree-planting *is* geo-engineering. My take is that geo-engineering means just that: the (ultra-hubristic) project of seeking to manage—to engineer, to plan, and to control top-down—the entire planet, the geosphere. Now, if what we do is, for example, grow vast (perhaps genetically-manipulated) forest-monocultures and then burn them and seek to sequester the carbon underground for hundreds of years, that would certainly count as an example of geo-engineering. And that's what is being planned. That is what BECCS is—BioEnergy with Carbon Capture and Storage. It's a little-known and terrifying fact that the Paris targets are premised on exactly that plan, to roll out

BECCS across huge swathes of the planet! I say 'terrifying' in part because there is very little reason indeed to suppose that the plan will work, even on its own terms.[21] We are gambling our planetary survival on technologies, such as this one, that either don't even exist yet or are merely at small-scale experimental pilot stage, or that we have reason to believe are dangerous, especially if they get scaled up.

But the right way to plant trees as a response to the climate threat is very different. It's to seek to restore biodiverse wild ecosystems; to recreate forests that used to be there (albeit tweaking what you seed, to reflect the coming temperature changes, etc.). It's rewilding, which means moving in the direction not of having to manage everything top-down but of no longer having to manage things. Rather, we intervene only in a way calculated to let nature regain control in the areas in question: we let the rivers flow again, let the trees return, and so forth. We create a situation where we then have to do *less*, not a situation where we have to seek to control ever more. We allow Nature her freedom.

This is not seeking to manage—to engineer—the planet. It's the opposite. It's removing our interferences with natural systems by taking out, for example, artificially-created grazing land and returning that land to how it was before we got too big for our boots. It means reinforcing and recreating, rather than diminishing, the Amazon rainforest—and every other real forest that we can regenerate.[22] It means restoring ecosystems and not, as some geo-engineering plans seek to do—such as the well-funded mainstream plans based in BECCS—converting yet more biodiverse ecosystems into fragile monocultures, 'green deserts', that will moreover be horribly vulnerable to burning up in the unprecedentedly terrible wildfires that global over-heat will bring us in the next generation or two.

Restoring natural systems, building down our interferences with large-scale processes, embodies the fundamental logic of precaution. The logic of the '*via negativa*': do less rather than always more; seek to facilitate resilient 'anti-fragile' systems; switch the burden of proof, such that anyone wanting to do something radically new needs to provide evidence that what they propose is safe, rather than us having to provide evidence that what they propose is harmful. It is particularly vital that this burden-shifting is effected, so far as geo-engineering is concerned, because, given that geo-engineering can only meaningfully be done at the planetary level, there is a real danger that its advocates are going to claim that there is no evidence that what they propose to do is harmful—until they have done it, by which time it will be too late to call out their recklessness!

Accordingly, the Precautionary Principle as I am using the phrase can be understood as follows: where there is a real risk of serious/irreversible harm, a lack of decisive evidence of that harm mustn't be used as a reason to prevaricate in guarding against the potential harm, and that, where the harm is catastrophic, this precautionary consideration ought to be considered absolute and decisive, no matter how nice the alleged benefits of the change in question.[23] In this sense the Precautionary Principle is or ought to be at the very basis of the emerging world-view that needs to supplant our ignorant and reckless technophilia and techno-optimism.

You are right, of course, Sam, that the clamour for geo-engineering will grow, as our climatic situation deteriorates. That deterioration is extremely likely to continue for a long time to come, of course, because of the time-lag of greenhouse gases staying in the atmosphere and the oceans having been warmed for decades or more, even in the unlikely event that we get our act together now and take mitigation seriously. But we should remain utterly unimpressed by that clamour for geo-engineering, for the reasons just outlined. The Precautionary Principle is precisely what we need to take seriously, at this time more than any other. It destroys the case for geo-engineering. Geo-engineering is nothing more than an extreme example of the very mind-set that has led us into the disastrous pass in which we find ourselves.

Furthermore, even if we were to light upon a form of geo-engineering that 'works', it would be outrageously irresponsible to create a dependency of our civilisation on such geo-engineering in any high-tech form. Because such dependency would mean that we had to gamble on successfully maintaining our high-tech civilisation indefinitely. That's an unacceptable gamble, given what we know about human fallibility, past societies' collapses, etc. Given that—to say the least—we can't be sure that we will achieve the civilisational transformation needed, it is reckless to build in dependence on any technology that requires continued human intervention to be workable, as geo-engineering would.

For the same reason, it is unacceptable to gamble on nuclear power, another ultra-high-technology, which creates waste that, unless carefully tended for hundreds of years, will prove fatally toxic in ways and at scales that events such as Chernobyl or Fukushima only begin to give the slightest sense of. Just try to picture what will happen if/when nuclear waste dumps and power plants around the world's coast—where they are virtually all located—get overwhelmed, in coming decades or centuries, by rising sea levels.

If for whatever reason our civilisation were to splutter or fail—and there are many possible reasons; climate is 'only' the most pressing of them—then our ability to maintain a successfully created geo-engineering scheme would obviously deteriorate or fail outright, at the same time. And this would probably lead to cataclysmic unprecedented sudden leaps in temperature; if, say, we suddenly stopped putting up the 'mirrors in space' that were artificially protecting us from global over-heat.[24]

We are going to have to learn to become, on balance, less dependent upon complex technologies. Such learning will either be voluntary, or we will suffer the consequences of extending our technological dependence too far into a future that we cannot control. Our fantasies of being able to control nature are exactly why we are in the predicament we are now in. The model of conquest of nature has proven cataclysmic.

To survive in any form, civilisation needs to become more precautious, not less.[25] If, as is overwhelmingly likely, our civilisation falls, then our remaining descendants will learn that lesson, in a hard way. It would be so much smarter if we could learn it first, in advance of collapse.

5. DEBATING CLIMATE CHANGE DENIERS—OR NOT?

SA: It could be argued that geo-engineering is only being discussed at all because the hard climate change denial of 'climate-sceptics', combined with the 'soft' climate change denial of the entire mainstream (denial of the scale and urgency of the problem), has prevented much meaningful action on climate, to date. As we were constructing this dialogue you provoked a social media storm by declining an invite to debate a 'hard' climate change denier on the BBC. Could you offer some insight into this event, what impact it had, and what motivated you to act as you did?

RR: One of the main reasons why this civilisation is finished and why collapse is now so likely is the rank failure of mass media to be honest about the horrific decline in biodiversity (i.e., in life on Earth) and about human-caused climate-decline being a white swan and a mortal threat. In my context of Great Britain, the BBC has been one of the worst culprits, in that, unlike newspapers, they have no excuse for not telling the truth, for they are supposed to be a public service broadcaster, not just a megaphone for powerful corporate interests. The BBC has, until very recently, seen 'balance' on the question of climate as a matter of 'He says, She says', i.e., as a matter simply of allowing climate scientists and those who accept what they are saying to debate as if as equals the closed-minded pseudo-science of climate-denialists. Until very recently, that is.

At the start of August 2018 I was telephoned by the BBC. Would I come on, in the context of the raging drought and other horrific climate-induced events of that summer in Greece, the USA, and many more, to debate the reality of anthropogenic dangerous climate change with a denier? My normal habit would have been to say 'Yes'. But before I could open my mouth, something else rose up within me, from my gut. A visceral distaste—and a call of conscience.

I just couldn't do it anymore. I couldn't pretend that there was any debate to be had with these pitiful and dangerous deniers. I couldn't stomach the absurdity of debating with them while the planet literally burns. I felt instead the same burning desire for truth and for honestly facing reality together that motivated our entire conversation, Sam.

So I said 'No'. I expressed my willingness to take part in lots of other debates about climate—for instance, Is the Paris Agreement enough? Are we on track for runaway climate change and civilisational collapse?—but not, any longer, to participate in the charade of debating these deeply dangerous jokers, the denialists.

That evening, I decided to send out a tweet on it. I thought: maybe what I've done, the little gesture of refusal I've made, might resonate with some people. I thought: maybe I'll even get 30 or 40 re-tweets out of this. Before I went to bed that night, I already had 1000 retweets. More than for any tweet I'd ever previously done, on anything, in ten years on Twitter. Next morning, I woke up to find that the tweet now had been shared 10,000 times. Clearly, I'd struck a chord.

I was then contacted by the BBC nationally, to get all the details straight. I started getting calls from the media not only in Britain, but also abroad. The story even made it to the *Sydney Morning Herald* in Australia. I was commissioned to write a *Guardian* op-ed, setting out my reasoning in detail for why we should boycott debates with denialists on the reality of climate chaos, and for why that would force a change of approach from broadcasters. I was contacted by the BBC Radio station that had sought to have me on, and they apologised and asked to meet with me. We discussed how they could avoid making the same mistake again; how they could have a discussion around climate that didn't flatter (i.e., that didn't need to include) the deniers.

Meanwhile that tweet just kept on growing. It was retweeted by some very notable names, including, most intriguingly of all, by Richard Sambrook, former Head of News at the BBC, who agrees—like many BBC journalists who contacted me privately—with what I had called for. It's now been shared by 42,000 people, liked by 60,000, and been seen by over 5 million people. This in itself is hugely encouraging: it shows how much people care about the media improving its act on climate and ecology.

I decided it was time to get a letter together of distinguished politicians, writers, and scientists, so that together we could put forward the same point of view: that the time for debate with denialists is past. The letter, signed by 60 of us, including Jonathon Porritt, Peter Tatchell, George Monbiot, and politicians from Labour, the LibDems and Greens, made a splash, appearing in print nationally.

Soon after that, a leaked memo emerged whose central point was that the BBC at last has accepted that it gets coverage of climate change 'wrong too often', and so it told staff: 'You do not need a "denier" to balance the debate.' *Exactly* what was at issue when I had got the call from the Beeb at the start of August, and said 'No'.

The lesson? Activism can work. But we ought not to get carried away with this result, obviously. All that's been achieved here is the most basic of acknowledgements of reality and scientific sense. The BBC still in no way takes climate nearly as seriously as it should.[26] The voices of those of us afraid that civilisation itself is now at risk of collapse still virtually never get heard. And hegemonic assumptions about 'growth', the culture of *more*, and so forth continue radically to undermine the prospects for meaningful action to prevent climatic disasters.

So, obviously, the story I've just told you is encouraging, especially by way of offering some hope that there might at last be a space opening up for uncompromising climate-honesty; but it does not alter the general diagnosis of our plight that is informing our discussion. Even after the elimination of hard climate denial, there indeed remains a soft denial that still mostly dominates the BBC and other media. A foolish forced effort to believe that business as usual can still mostly go on as is.

6. THE GOD OF GREEN GROWTH HAS FORSAKEN US

SA: Such 'soft denial' seems especially ubiquitous in connection with our domination by conventional economic ideas that should surely be recognised now as outdated. Earlier we were speaking of techno-optimism, which is perhaps most influential in the domain of macroeconomics. Through this lens, techno-optimism could be re-defined as the belief that the problems caused by economic growth can be solved by more 'growth' (as measured by GDP), provided we learn how to produce and consume more efficiently through the application of science, technology, and better design. Could it be that economic growth is now causing the problems economic growth is expected to solve? Can this paradox be resolved? 'Green growth' is widely held up as the solution to our planetary woes, and yet as this goal is pursued, we see the face of Gaia vanishing.

RR: 'Green growth' sounds great, doesn't it? Like 'clean coal', maybe... But perhaps we are starting to learn by now that if something sounds too good to be true, then it probably is.

Why do we value growth at all? Because we value economic activity; at least *valuable* economic activity. (In fact, much of what GDP measures is valueless or indeed worse than nothing, such as most financial speculation; and meanwhile it leaves out a great deal that is valuable, such as much caring work).[27] But, while it may have made sense to have economic growth at certain moments in history—when the volume of economic activity was easily containable within the limits of our ecology, and if some people's most basic needs for sustenance were not being met—we are largely no longer in such a world. The world we live in is a 'full' world. Its central problems are the greed of those running the show and the degrading of ecosystems. We need to share far more equally what we have; but we also need to recognise that the idea that we have high or even inexhaustible material needs is itself an ideological assumption that needs unmasking and rejecting.

The world moreover has too many people in it to be safe, especially given that a growing number of those people (nearly everyone, in countries such as the UK and Australia) are over-consuming, and a smaller number are over-consuming at levels of such decadence that Roman Emperors would blush. In such a world, more human activity (more economic activity overall, etc.) *is not a good thing.*

Firstly, because we (by which I mean here most human beings in this civilisation) are too busy as it is (except for the minority who, while most of us are over-worked and over-stressed, face enforced labourlessness); and too much of our time is spent in the economy (rather than in contemplation, or in wilderness, or making love...). Let's share out the work that needs to be done more intelligently (i.e., more equally), but let's also strive to simply abjure much work that oughtn't to be done at all. Less frenetic human activity would be better *in itself*, even regardless of the ecological consequences of excess human activity. Let's have *wiser* human activity. That will include: there being less of it. But not just less of the same; less and different. We should not support dreams that point in the opposite direction to this wisdom. Many human dreams have become thoroughly infected by materialism, myths of 'progress', etc. Real progress would be something very different, and perhaps later we could return to this issue and consider what it might look like.

For now, let me focus explicitly on the ecological dimension. Unless you 'angelise' economic activity, eliminating its environmental impact altogether—which there is no reason to believe is possible—then increasing economic activity is *prima facie* now a dangerous thing to encourage. There is almost nothing we do in the economy that literally has 'zero marginal cost'.[28] Even humble individual emails have a small but real cost in terms of energy and materials; and when billions of them get sent, that cost adds up to a very large one, systemically. It follows that ever-increasing levels of economic activity are incompatible with a finite planet. That means that eventually there are limits, like it or not, to how much we can and should produce. The green-growthist fantasy is just the same old 'Prometheanism'[29] in disguise; it still implies that there are no limits that humans cannot overcome.

But not only are there limits, we have *breached* them already; that is why this civilisation is finished, running off the cliff with its feet in the air like those old cartoon characters we grew up with. We cannot endlessly expand the economy and still be green; it's oxymoronic. We can't keep growing the cake when the ingredients are running out and the kitchen is filling with smoke. There are *no* extant examples of economies reducing their footprints sufficiently to achieve one-planet-living per-capita levels. Actual reductions in levels of economic activity are needed.[30]

As leading green economists Peter Victor and Tim Jackson have shown,[31] the rapid reductions in overall ecological footprint that we need in order to live as if we only had one planet are not compatible, according to our best models, with any net-economic-growth-paths *at all*. So, if a proposed trajectory coincides with net economic growth, then it is not genuinely green. If someone says of overall economic growth/GDP that it might go up 'in a green way' then they are wrong. While it is true to say that we want the renewables sector to grow, for example, this is only tenable if other sectors (e.g., fossil fuels and nuclear) *shrink more*. So this means: no *net* growth, and eventually 'degrowth'[32] (and 'eventually' must now be very soon!).

It is crucial that we resist growth*ism*, the very widespread drive to keep the economy 'growing'.[33] For (perpetual) growthism is a perpetual obstacle to collective sanity, to facing the reality of limits. Growthism endlessly makes it *harder* for us to stop breaching our planet's limits, and to start looking the future calmly and honestly in the eye in the way that we are seeking to do in this dialogue. And green growthism is merely a subset of growthism.

In an era where it is clear that social and ecological limits to growth are being breached, the over-arching question should be: Can we afford more growth? The answer is clear: No. But progress on these points being understood is glacially slow. Way too slow to expect enough change on the kind of timetable we need. It still seems, tragically, far more likely that growth will end because of collapse than because of informed decision.

7. CIVIL DISOBEDIENCE AND THE EXTINCTION REBELLION

SA: That is a fair, though dark, diagnosis of our collective situation, and—if I may shift from economics to politics—it probably calls for a fundamental revision of the Marxian theory of change. Whereas Marx foresaw a time when the proletariat would rise up and replace capitalism by way of revolution, what looks to be the more likely course of events is that capitalism is replaced not by way of revolution but by way of collapse. And even if the Marxist revolution comes first, then collapse lies ahead all the same unless socialists adopt a post-growth position too. Currently, it seems most socialists remain entrenched in the growth paradigm as much as capitalists, which is unfortunate to say the least. You will be familiar with Edward Abbey's provocative but painfully apt quip that 'growth for the sake of growth is the ideology of the cancer cell'. Whether that is capitalist growth or socialist growth, the underlying cancer is fatal all the same, eating away at the biosphere upon which the entire community of life depends for our mutual co-existence.

RR: That's why Ted Kaczynski, the uncompromising political thinker whose best-known claim to fame is his former identity as the Unabomber,[34] makes the discomforting and difficult-to-refute argument (in his *Manifesto*) that socialism is the leading edge of the disastrous doctrines of 'progress' and 'growth'. It is what enables those dogmas to be able to dress themselves up with a patina of respectability.

SA: Yes, and so the ecocidal economics of growth works with similar fatality whether in its Left or Right forms; fatal, you've argued, for our civilisation, and fatal for our non-human kin. We're in the process of decimating wildlife and insect populations across the world. As we were having the conversation, a report was published by the WWF which highlighted the extent of ecological violence that flows from our human activity. After assessing 4,000 species of birds, mammals, fish, and reptiles, the WWF report concluded grimly that the populations of these vertebrate species had declined on average by 60% since 1970. You will also be familiar with the German study published in 2017 which concluded that insect biomass has declined by an alarming 75% over the last three decades. Let us dwell on those harrowing statistics for a moment.

RR: When I'm giving talks these days, I sometimes ask the audience to join me in a minute's silence to reflect on these mind-bending, horrendous facts. The quality of the silence is often of a rare and profound nature. We need to really take in, deep inside ourselves, what our civilisation has been built on. The rape and murder of most nature.

SA: The term 'the 6th mass extinction' is barely adequate to the situation. After all, none of the previous five were the result of the actions of one, supposedly intelligent species. What is perhaps most challenging is that this ecological devastation is occurring half a century or more after the birth of the modern environmental movement. It seems that environmental activism to date has won occasional battles but is decidedly losing the war. It prompts one to reflect on whether activist strategies historically might have been misconceived. Might a new environmental activism be required? In fact, I pose that question at a time when something called the Extinction Rebellion has erupted in the United Kingdom, where you reside, and I understand you have been intimately involved in this rebellion, which is engaging in non-violent acts of civil disobedience. Could you explain what the Extinction Rebellion (aka 'XR') is and share your experiences as a participant in this social uprising.

RR: One of the wonderful things about XR, as you imply, is that it is a movement that is starting to escape the death-grip of humanism, the anthropocentrism that has been hegemonic for far too long. In XR, we focus first and foremost on climate-breakdown as the most pressing existential threat to the Earth-ecosystem, but we focus too on the stupid, criminal, and heartless elimination of most of the world's biodiversity as a catastrophe also for us, for that ecosystem, and above all of course for the beings who are being rendered extinct (i.e., killed, murdered). The 'Extinction' in our title refers inter alia to humans, but by no means only to humans. It refers also to the other beings we are already rendering extinct at extreme rates. Our Rebellion is against their Extinction, not just against our own!

When I contemplate the fact that within my lifetime more than half of life on Earth has been eliminated, by my species, I feel a great horror and a great shame. If one really contemplates this fact, I don't believe that one can carry on living comfortably within this system. One has no alternative but to rebel.

And that's one reason why, as soon as I found out that XR was going to be launched, I sought out its founders and threw myself into it. XR and its initial growth and successes are one of the most potent reasons for having faith that civilisational transformation might yet be possible, that an uncontrolled collapse (rather than a 'controlled demolition' and substitution) of this civilisation is not yet quite inevitable. (Another example is the Climate Strike movement among children begun by the inspirational Greta Thunberg, who I had the great privilege of eulogising when she spoke from the platform at the 1st XR launch event at Parliament Square in London on 31 October 2018).

The demands of the Extinction Rebellion are 'impossible' demands. They are simply not reconcilable with even a reformed version of politics or economics as usual. They could only be accommodated by putting in process a revolutionary transformation in our entire way of life. This is most clearly visible on the demand for the UK to go carbon-neutral by 2025. This would/will require a drastic path of energy descent. Not even 'just' the kind of thing envisaged, rightly, by the Transition Towns movement; for my country to go to net zero carbon within six years, that will require most carbon-dependent activities to be simply phased out during this time-period. Not to be replaced like for like by renewables-powered alternatives—that's not possible.[35]

In simple, concrete terms: this target will mean that many of our fossil power stations simply have to be shut down. And many of our cars and lorries simply mothballed (rather than replaced with shiny 'green' electric cars or whatever). This is the kind of thing that is now needed, in order to achieve climate-safety. (For the IPCC goals are not safe, not even the 1.5 degree programme,[36] and 'developed' countries such as the UK need to lead the way in dropping the carbon drug, kicking the carbon habit.) It is almost but not quite unimaginable. It is unimaginable unless we are willing to enter a new 'imaginary'.

It is only conceivable, that is, if we achieve a change in consciousness; if *many* of us dare to feel in our hearts, to imagine and swiftly to strive for a different civilisation, one founded in precaution, and junking the endless quest for 'more'.

We need to look our climate emergency and the extinction emergency in the face, unflinchingly. Honesty and seriousness—and just possibly saving the future—then demands precisely the kind of 'revolutionary' goals that XR has, and precisely the kind of 'revolutionary' means that it posits in order to achieve those goals.

The hope that remains to us, after we have accepted that reformist efforts have failed and that we are on a white swan trajectory toward collapse—and if we are to have any chance of achieving civilisational transformation—is that, when we face this dark climate-reality, we will find the courage to act on it; to do enough, to transform our society and ourselves and to adapt to the changed climate and potential collapse that the coming generation(s) will inevitably harbour. When the bad that humanity has unleashed is faced, then we can rise up to meet and equalise and overcome it. This is a spiritual and an ecological hope, as much as a political one. Our spirit needs to be as strong as the reality is dire. If it truly is, if our state of consciousness tracks the state of the world, then there is a sense in which, however badly wrong things have gone, we are *ready* to right them. The catastrophe we have unleashed then in turn unleashes *us*: the saving power.

Will XR succeed? Its task is far harder than the precedents that get cited for it, such as the civil rights movement. It is challenging our whole way of life. It requires us to be willing to become 'poorer'—i.e., in material terms; we'll be richer in terms of community, of the life of the spirit, of access to nature and wilderness. And, of course, ultimately we'll be richer materially, too, than we would be on our present path—because that is a path toward collapse. There are no jobs in a civilisation that has vanished.

It would be a very brave person who would bet on XR's victory. But the more of us who are willing to become part of this rising-up, of course, the more possible such 'impossible' but necessary victory becomes. And, if we fail, then at least we will have tried. The thing that would be really intolerable, so shaming that it would be hard to square with life going on at all, would be if we reached (say) 2030, and the world was tipping into runaway catastrophic climate change or a terminal breakdown of ecosystems, and we couldn't look our kids in the face and tell them that at least we really fully tried to salvage their future.

We have to risk our full selves. We have to try, without reservation.

8. POLITICS AND SPIRITUALITY

SA: It is risky business to talk about 'spiritual matters', especially among green-minded persons, many of whom these days tend to be rigorously secular. What do you mean by 'spirit' when you say we'll be 'richer in terms of the life of the spirit'?

RR: It seems obvious to me that our profound civilisational crisis is not only political-economic, but also psychological, philosophical, ethical, and, yes, spiritual. I don't mean by that to invoke any mumbo-jumbo—now is the time for (inter alia) ecological science to take precedence. What I mean is that the crisis goes to the very roots and core of our being and of the meaning of our lives, and that it calls for a response not limited to intellection nor to practical action nor to the scientific worldview. In the urgency of the challenge we face we are called, also, to slow down and reflect deeply. We are called upon to appreciate the beauty and peace in every moment—because, not knowing how long we have, we need to enjoy it while it lasts. This is always so for human beings, as all great wisdom traditions have taught; but how much more so in an era in which, tragically, the very continuity of human existence can no longer be taken for granted. We are called upon to be *present* in the travail of our times, to face reality fully as a conscientious meditator does. When I talk about spirituality, I mean simply being willing to consider that the kind of 'mystical' insight into our connectedness and our wholeness that some of us find through meditation (or through being in wild nature, or through prayer, or through being part of an affinity group, or through various other means) is not exhausted by the results of reductionist neuroscientific inquiry.

Such insight is deeply important, in the crisis that we find ourselves in, both for its own sake and because of the strength it could unleash.

For when collectively we accept that we are now highly vulnerable to self-destruction, we are *for that very reason* potentially more open to loving life (in all its simplicity and complexity) than ever before. Seeing the vulnerability of ourselves and our living world clearly for the first time opens us to its beauty properly, as if for the first time. This is both a wonderful gift in itself (we can experience a deeper joy than we've ever known before, even if—should we fail—it might end up being fleeting) *and* a potentially powerful mode of access to our full power as an uprising. For when we see and feel the beauty of humanity and of 'Gaia' adequately for the first time, then we have little choice but to *rise up and defend it* adequately (for the first time...).

There is a further benefit that comes with such an emphasis on the far greater importance to us ultimately of the pursuit of wisdom and the—engaged, active, serious—life of the spirit compared to the life of material gratification. Namely, that when we experience the precedence of spiritual over material wealth, we are better placed to be motivated to reduce the size of our footprint. This is a time in history when there is a very great collective benefit potentially consequent upon storing treasures in our hearts, rather than in the stock exchange.

SA: You spoke earlier of how anthropocentric humanism could be understood as an attempt to replace religion as we have known it historically with a kind of self-worship, a narcissism of humanity. You implied that this was dangerous in part because it risked losing what was of value in religion(s). You are now clearly carving out a place for spirituality. And religion? And religious *faith*? Should this too be welcomed into a picture of an alternative to our failed civilisation and to 'Empire'?

RR: Almost certainly—but let me clarify that statement. I suspect that we will see the rise of a kind of Earth-centred or nature-centred pantheism as people start to realise, as this civilisation disintegrates, how perilous it is to regard nothing save perhaps our present-day selves (and our machines?) as sacred.[37] Some go further, and suggest that a form of animism, still alive today not just among indigenous peoples but considerably more widely, is actually what is poised to return.[38]

But look, let's be open and tolerant about this; let's not risk starting some kind of sectarian fight or getting lost in speculations. You and I don't need to decide whether to plump for pantheism (though I would recommend its virtues) or animism or something else. It's a mistake to see faith as limited to spirituality or religion alone. The concept of faith can and should play a key role hereabouts in either a spiritual *or* a secular[39] version of the kind of move made by philosopher William James, with his concept of the 'will to believe'.

James suggests that, when it comes to commitment to matters of ultimate import, there is just no question of being able to approach them in a thoroughly 'evidence-based' way. There are matters that ultimately go 'beyond' evidence, or where evidence is in the end imponderable. There are matters where our agency, our willpower, *itself* can be decisive. When I say, for example, that it is very unlikely that this civilisation will transform itself for the better and survive, there is a sense in which what I say is necessarily misleading; because *it is up to us*. Strictly speaking, probabilities don't apply; because we can't find out what is going to happen by merely observing, nor by doing a scientific experiment. We can only find out by doing (it), by living, by acting. You aren't a spectator to what is unfolding. You are part of it. The more people who join Extinction Rebellion or the climate school strikes, and (perhaps) the more people who read and act on this book, the more hope gets generated that we might yet change course.

This is encouraging. It means that however bad the odds against us get, if hope remains in us then hope really does remain. For there never really are, strictly speaking, *odds* at all; we operate within very real biological and physical constraints that we have been terrible at recognising let alone respecting, but these never doom us, provided there is any room for manoeuvre left.

So we need to have a certain faith in ourselves,[40] to believe in ourselves, to trust in our potentiality, *despite our pretty terrible record*. It would be fatal if our focussing on that record and our being realistic about how the deck is stacked against us now, were to eliminate that faith. We need to feel a confidence: that a change of course remains eminently *possible.*

If we assume that we are doomed, then we will definitely be doomed. If we believe that transformation remains possible, and that any collapse-event will be better or worse depending upon what we believe and upon what we choose to do, on how we prepare, then that belief will be to some extent at least vindicated.

This makes this choice clear and almost easy.

9. RESOLVING POVERTY: 'DEVELOPMENT' OR POST-DEVELOPMENT?

SA: In answering recent questions you've mentioned the contrast between spiritual and material riches, and of the need, implicit in XR, for a kind of shared voluntary poverty or voluntary simplicity. This prompts me to return to a comment you made earlier and flesh it out a bit, because it touches on a critical issue. It concerns poverty and the desire to live in a world where humanity's basic needs for sustenance are universally and securely met, in a way that is consistent with ecological limits. You seemed to question the idea that historically most people's basic needs were not met. I want to press you on this a little bit so I can better understand your position.

RR: I don't think it's true that historically the basic needs for sustenance of most people were not met. Or at least, certainly not *pre*historically; things tended to change, on balance for the worse, after the agricultural revolution, but even (since) then, many peasants have carved out perfectly good ways of living (lightly) on the Earth, provided that they weren't savagely oppressed by overlords.

SA: From my reading of the historical situation, it is certainly true that there were agrarian or hunter-gatherer subsistence economies around the world in which societies met their basic needs simply and relatively securely, and which may not deserve the label of 'poverty' even though their material living standards were extremely low by modern standards in affluent societies. However, I believe it remains the case that throughout history there were also significant portions of the global population that lived insecure and destitute lives— lives which can and should be properly described as miserable and poverty-stricken and utterly incompatible with a full and dignified human existence. I do not wish to glorify the present, but I would caution against romanticising the past with too broad a brush.

RR: Of course, romanticisation is to be avoided;[41] but we must equally beware of the massive tendency in our world today to assume that we have 'progressed' uniformly from the past, and that the past was always a time of hardship compared to today (at least to what people such as you and I experience today). I have become very sceptical of the story we tell ourselves about 'progress'. I've been influenced by Wittgenstein, by David Ehrenfeld, John Gray, Ronald Wright, and Helena Norberg-Hodge—as well as by much indigenous thought—toward thinking that actually the idea that we have progressed is in certain key respects delusional.

In particular, I want to suggest that for most of human history, and in particular for most of the pre-agricultural age (bearing in mind that the agricultural age is still only a tiny fraction of our species' history), most of humanity has lived a pretty easy and good life. It is only likely to be true that throughout *recorded* history there were, as you claim, 'significant portions of the global population that lived insecure and destitute lives'. Hunter-gatherers (or perhaps 'gatherer-hunters', as it appears that in many cases the majority of their calories came from the gathering) really were, as Marshall Sahlins puts it, the original affluent societies, and even the original leisure societies. Not having to invest vast amounts of time in growing food, they (have) tended to live well (*'buen vivir'*!), keeping fit naturally while having plenty of time to sit around the campfire.

Am I proposing that we go back to living as they did? Of course not; and it's impossible, in any case, there being too many of us. But am I proposing we seek humbly to learn from them, and (crucially) from the remaining indigenous peoples, and especially hunter-gatherer peoples, the 'earth-keepers' as they are sometimes called? Absolutely I am.

SA: OK, but it nevertheless seems to me that around the world today—despite several centuries of capitalist 'development'—there are literally billions who are, by any humane standard, under-consuming. This includes those people whose bodies suffer the devastating effects of malnutrition and who are literally on the brink of starvation—by some estimates we are talking here of 800 million people or so, in countries like Ethiopia, Haiti, and the Congo. But it also includes billions of others who lack access to basic systems of safe sanitation and drinking water, and whose lives could be greatly improved by increasing their material living standards through more secure access to healthy food in decent proportions, better tools, basic medicines, safer cooking technologies, etc.

The fact that there were materially sufficient subsistence economies in history must not be used to deflect attention away from the fact that capitalism is destroying those ways of life and leaving genuine, unromantic destitution in its place. Jason Hickel is an authority on global poverty today and by his reckoning there are more than four billion people whose material living standards are insufficient to meet basic nutritional needs and achieve a normal life expectancy. This is a great blow to the 'good news narrative' of capitalist development as espoused by the World Bank, the IMF, and prominent defenders of 'progress' like Steven Pinker.

So I guess, to me, it seems that there are literally billions of people around the world whose material living standards are so low and insecure that an increase in those material living standards would better achieve the vision of a civilisation in which everyone has 'enough' to live a full and dignified human existence. Of course, 'development' as we know it today is not the path to poverty resolution and in fact development is arguably more often responsible for (re)producing it. Likewise, turning the Global South into the Global North would be utterly catastrophic, especially ecologically. I am far more sympathetic with the 'post-development' school of thought that seeks localised sufficiency economies that evolve in culturally and context specific ways; but the point remains: resolving poverty and achieving 'sufficiency' for all may well imply increased overall demands on already over-burdened planetary ecosystems, which provides a further compelling reason for the richest nations to give up their pursuit of ever-increasing material living standards by way of economic growth, and indeed, initiate a degrowth process of planned economic contraction.

Perhaps you could further unpack your position on poverty and how you see it being resolved in a post-growth world.

RR: There's much of course that I agree with you on wholeheartedly here, Sam. In particular, I think that Pinker's narrative of the alleged 'decline of violence' is a delusion and a disgrace, and I am glad that the huge flaws in it have been shown up graphically by Ed Herman, Nassim Taleb, and others.

Now, in some ways I would just love to agree with you completely. It would be wonderfully convenient if we could imagine a post-growth egalitarian future in which 'contraction and convergence' had occurred worldwide, and everyone had something like what our society regards as enough.

But there are two central and devastating problems with this, and these require me to take up once again your invitation at the start of our conversation to a relentless honesty, no matter what conclusions it leads to. First, as we've already discussed, I am convinced that we are facing an ending of our civilisation which will rapidly make this dream impossible. And, tragically, that ending is much more likely to come via collapse than via a peaceful transformation to something very different from what we have, from what can be sustained. And there is a danger that if we keep encouraging the so-called 'developing' world to keep 'developing'—and the use of words like 'under-consuming' encourages exactly that—we are simply making collapse more certain, and turning the coming vast change into a likely climatic-and-more cataclysm.

Second, I am in any case unconvinced that it would be *desirable* for everyone to attain even something like the 'standard of living' that people have in countries like Cuba or Costa Rica, two of the very few countries in the world today that it might possibly be argued are managing to achieve both ecological sustainability and some measure of economic justice.

Let me explain the second point. A huge influence on me here is Helena Norberg-Hodge, whose book *Ancient Futures* is I guess a sort of bible of serious post-development thinking—and deservedly so. I believe, as I've written in the pieces I've co-published with Helena, that it is completely unacceptable for us to conceive of ourselves as having achieved a superior mode of existence to hunter-gatherer and to certain peasant societies. Rather, we should aim to foster a post-growthist relocalisation that deliberately looks beyond most of what we take for granted in the 'developed' world.

I agree with you that hundreds and perhaps thousands of millions of people in the world today, and throughout the agricultural age in fact, are living lives that involve destitution, and that this is morally wrong. But I no longer believe that the solution to this primarily involves seeking to 'lift up' these people. I think that their destitution is a *product* of our system and in particular of its tendency to destroy real communities and to generate vast inequality. I think we ought to be thinking about how to dismantle the system, much more than about how to 'share the wealth'.

So when you say that 'around the world today—despite several centuries of capitalist "development"—there are literally billions who are, by any humane standard, under-consuming', I would reframe that, fairly radically, as follows: I would say that 'around the world today—because of several centuries of capitalist development—there are literally billions who are poor *because there are others who are rich*.' I don't think that most of the world's poor need more dollars. I think what they need is for the rich to be expropriated—i.e., simply for inequality to be radically reduced, even if that means that everyone has less material 'goods'—and for society to be put back on a footing where communities are much more self-reliant, and where people can largely provide for themselves from the land, oceans, and so on.

What is sometimes helpfully called, in the words of my Green House thinktank colleague Molly Scott Cato MEP, a 'bioregional economy', or a provisioning economy.

Creating such an economy is one of the ways we might conceivably yet avoid collapse. It will also make those within it far more resilient against the consequences of any collapse. It will require a philosophy of what I call 'enoughism'; the end of the culture of (always) 'more'. Enoughism is a concept about what and how little, economically speaking, human *needs* are.

The very idea of us as 'consumers' is part of the problem, not of the solution. The world's poor mostly do not need to consume more; they do not need to be richer than those of their (our) peasant and indigenous forebears who enjoyed what I call a 'rich subsistence'. They (and we!) need lives that make sense, in real communities, with some security. They need what most people throughout most of history have had, and what Helena depicts in the first part of her splendid book.

Many of the world's poor now look enviously upon what we have. The answer is not to try, futilely (because the planetary limits will not allow it) to 'lift them up'; it is for us to give up most of what we have; and for us to explain that we are in any case not all that we are cracked up to be (to point out, for example, the ferocious epidemics of mental ill-health ravaging the world's North today).[42] The answer is to look and to lead beyond the dead-end that is our civilisation, not to try to enfold everyone within that civilisation's grip of death.

In fact, if, as appears highly likely, this civilisation suffers an at-least-partial collapse, then this may have certain good consequences, amidst the general horror and transitional devastation. Foremost among those consequences may be a substantial levelling; that the absurd fortunes of the rich and the super-rich, especially those fortunes that exist largely electronically, will be wiped out.[43]

Clearly this 'programme' for a relocalised world is a radical one. The real question perhaps then becomes: how much 'First World' way of living, and in particular our technology, can or *should* survive the end of this civilisation?

10. TECHNOLOGY AFTER EMPIRE

SA: Interesting, that's worth digging into a little deeper. How can we preserve some (desirable) technologies in and through the Great Disruption that may well be coming? Can we learn to be less dependent upon technology or some technologies? These are confronting questions, especially in an age when most people seem to assume we need more technology, not less. I am of the view that humanity already has all the technology it needs to solve all our problems. Lack of technology is not our problem—what we are doing with the technology we have is our problem, and that poses an ethical challenge far more than a technocratic or engineering challenge. In short, how much of our technology can or should survive the collapse of civilisation as we know it?

RR: I'm a philosopher, so my response to this vital question begins, as much of my thinking does, in a fundamentally precautionary approach. I still think we should strive to 'transformationally adapt' our civilisation; that is, while accepting that we have already damaged our climate and biodiversity in appalling and partly-irreparable ways, and that this will get worse for some time to come even if we achieve an unparalleled consciousness-shift rapidly, we should seek to aim for civilisational transformation. We should seek to restore biodiverse ecosystems (including for instance wetlands, rather than building carbon-heavy and brittle 'conventional' flood defences), to permaculturise agriculture, to be fleet and flexible in our plantings and our seed-selection, and so forth.

But we need to be prepared for the worst: including the strong possibility that transformative adaptation will not happen, or will not happen fast enough. Thus, as the ultimate insurance policy, we also need 'deep adaptation'. We need to prepare our societies for being able to cope with collapse. That's what deep adaptation is: adaptation that is premised on the possibility or indeed probability of such collapse.

One key implication of the deep adaptation agenda is the following fact: it's profoundly irresponsible, at this moment in history, to foster any technology that requires ongoing high-tech or high-organisational inputs in order to remain safe. I argued earlier that this already rules out most forms of geo-engineering, certainly including 'Solar Radiation Management' (mirrors in space, etc.: for, if these were relied upon but then couldn't be maintained because of a civilisational failure, that—the sudden climate shock resulting—would be worse than if they hadn't been put in place at all). I also mentioned earlier that I believe that this now rules out nuclear power. Nuclear power is often talked up as a would-be 'answer' to the wicked problem of carbon-emissions-driven climate-damage. But once one starts to think through what will happen to nuclear power stations and nuclear waste if and when civilisation goes down, then it becomes starkly clear how utterly irresponsible it is to build any new nuclear. And we need to move to shut down and make safe nuclear facilities, the world over. Lest they melt down when they are no longer adequately maintained. Or lest their waste (especially their radioactive spent fuel rods) boils inadequately-maintained cooling ponds dry, and then ignites, burning terrible toxic fires into our atmosphere for decades or even centuries.

Hitherto, we've put nearly all of our eggs in prevention/mitigation baskets, so far as climate is concerned. That's no longer a tenable project. Global over-heat and climate chaos are here to stay and to worsen; so, insofar as it is possible to do so, we must seek to adapt to them. The hegemonic culture reaches for shallow-adaptation 'solutions' that enable us to continue to live in a more or less unchanged way: such as building bigger sea walls. These are not only likely to fail in the long term, but they actually worsen the prevention/mitigation situation, by requiring big and ongoing carbon emissions in order to implement. Such 'shallow adaptation' is clearly worse than inadequate. I call it maladaptive adaptation.

Thus the need for 'transformative adaptation': we need to look for 'win-wins', stratagems of adaptation that simultaneously mitigate and help directly to transform our civilisation in the way that it needs to be transformed. But, as I've said, even that isn't enough; for we have to be brave enough to consider that failure is very possible, even overwhelmingly likely: thus we cannot dodge the need for deep adaptation. We need to start making safe the waste products of nuclear and other technologies that will be profoundly hazardous to future civilisations—unless we make them safe.

Another criterion: technologies ought to be assessed primarily not in terms of their capacity for profit, nor even for making our lives 'easier', but for ecological viability and for *conviviality*. This is the term used by the brilliant Ivan Illich. We should want technologies that work as part of the lives we might live together as long-term flourishing communities; technologies that bring us together, that we can manage, that don't require militarisation, and so forth. Nuclear fails again, on this front, as Illich himself argued in his marvellous little book *Tools for conviviality*.

And finally, technology should be subservient to society's democratic will.[44] This final criterion can be found in the work of the great political philosopher Hannah Arendt. Any technology that subverts such a will, and can force a society to adapt to it rather than vice versa, is *prima facie* bad. An example I gave earlier is GMOs, which can easily displace (by 'infecting') traditional organic agriculture.

So I'd modify slightly but significantly what you said in your question, Sam. You said that 'humanity already has all the technology it needs to solve all our problems'. I'd respond that humanity has more than enough technology; it has in fact too much. Of course we should be looking for new technologies that can be genuinely helpful in our existential crisis; but we should be looking on balance to reduce our dependence upon technology, not increase it. Technology is not going to solve all our problems; and some of our technologies—and in particular the outsized hopes we have for them—*are* the problem.

11. THE 'INFORMATION DEFICIT' MODEL OF CHANGE

SA: Your suggestion that technology should be made subservient to society's 'democratic will' might strike some as too optimistic. It would be nice to look back, in a few decades' time, and see that the transition to an ecological civilisation was smooth and rational; that individuals, communities, nations, and even the globe came together to shape collective decisions with sensible, evidence-based reasoning and compassionate, democratic politics. But didn't we more or less have all the information and evidence we needed to change our destructive ways back in the 70s? Rachel Carson's *Silent Spring* was out; the *Limits to Growth* publication was sparking debate; Andre Gorz was talking about the need for 'degrowth', and so forth. For decades it has been clear that the growth economies of industrial civilisation are dangerously undermining the ecosystems that the entire community of life depends on to flourish. And yet, on reflection, we see that the global economy has resembled a snake eating its own tail, seemingly unaware that it is consuming its own life-support system.

So who still thinks a new 'theory' or 'report' is going to change things? Who thinks we lack evidence? That we don't have enough information to justify fundamentally changing course? These questions, of course, are rhetorical. The evidence is in, and yet Empire marches on. This is a very challenging conclusion to arrive at, especially for people like us, who are in the business of argument, evidence, and reasoning.

As academics we have a self-interest in adopting the 'information deficit' model of change, which essentially holds that when human beings are sufficiently well informed, they will make good decisions that advance wellbeing, justice, and sustainability. If human beings are making bad decisions, then it must be because they are not sufficiently informed. Therefore, according to this theory of change, we scientists and theoreticians just need to provide more information, clearer arguments, better evidence, because human beings are rational and they will eventually adjust their decisions, voting practices, and worldviews to reflect the best available evidence. Ha!

I'm not sure many people ever subscribed to this view in its purest form –

RR: Actually, let me interrupt you there, Sam, because I think actually quite a lot of us *did*, at least until 10 or 20 years ago. Especially, I think that natural scientists, who are mostly not used to thinking about people's minds in a sophisticated way, thought this. They thought they could present us with the evidence of pollution, of extinctions, and so forth, and we would change. And there are even a few examples where they seemed to be proved right in this assumption: such as in the case of the 'ozone hole'. (Though note that, even in that case, it was only once the clever, inaccurate metaphor of an ozone *hole* was dreamed up that the ozone crisis was acted upon.) But by and large the information deficit model of change has proven a pretty catastrophic failure.

In fact, arguably there is an information *surplus* in our world. What is lacking is wisdom, which is something completely different.

SA: Exactly. Just providing information about what's going wrong and what could be done better doesn't seem to be working at all; it doesn't seem to be an effective strategy for change. We all have a self-image of being rational and evidence-based in our thinking and reasoning, and yet one only needs to look at the world to see that such a self-image is not reflected in reality. So I, too, have grave doubts about the information deficit model of change. It seems to be applying a rational worldview to an irrational species—and yet giving up on evidence and reasoning is surely not the answer.

To what extent do you think new information, better evidence, and sound reasoning will spark the changes that are needed? If we shouldn't rely primarily on that rationalistic mode of societal change, from where will the sparks of deep transition ignite?

RR: Your point about not giving up on evidence and reasoning is of course essential. Those who want to turn this into a post-truth world—whether we are talking about purveyors of climate-denying pseudo-science, or about certain extreme 'post-modernists' or 'relativists', or about the 'leader of the free world' (sic)—need firmly pushing back against. We need to stand up for science, for preserving civil spaces of real argument and dialogue, for a media that cares about the difference between fake and real news. We need of course to unmask those who fund lies of all kinds, in pursuit of their short-term profit. But that's not enough. Nowhere near.

We need also to create a larger space for honest philosophical and ethical reflection. We might start by teaching the good life (and that means, among other things, teaching philosophy!) in schools more. As they do in much of continental Europe. But even that's not enough. Still nowhere near.

As your question perhaps implies, we need, like in *The Hunger Games*, to spark *the catching of a fire*. And that is more likely to be done by way of actual noble sacrifices (an eco-Jesus? A hunger-strike by the younger generation whose futures are being eaten?); or of inspirational authenticities (such as that of Petra Kelly, founder of the German Green Party, meeting whom was one of the defining and life-changing events of my youth); or of *stories*, rather than mainly by way of anything taught in universities.

In this context, the box-office smash-hit that was *Avatar* has greatly inspired me.[45] Here is a film with a 'message' of the kind we need; and it is nothing less than the most successful film of all time (despite having been banned in rural China, because the dictatorship there feared, rightly, that it might spark environmental revolts against land-grabbing).[46]

To generalise from this: we need narratives; it's a crime that there hasn't yet been a single major TV drama series exploring (say) both catastrophic *and* less bad scenarios *vis-à-vis* climate. And we need intelligent *reframing* of the issues:[47] the entire field of language needs ploughing over, to overcome the mind- and life-destroying power of words such as 'growth', 'progress', 'development', 'humanism', and instead to highlight (for instance) the possibility of one-planet living, and the beautiful coincidence that the very things we need to do in order to arrest climate chaos would be the very things we need to do in order to live happier, more locally-rooted, richer, more secure lives.

Perhaps we need an environmental Pearl Harbour. Something so big and undeniable that it wakes people up en masse. We must be careful what we wish for, of course. It's awful to even have to contemplate that our best hope for civilisational transformation in time may now lie in something truly awful happening. But one thing we should talk about—let's come back to this—is how disasters, in their horror, may carry a silver lining; how they might *turn* the crisis we are in into an opportunity.

However; none of what I have been describing is a matter of *irrationality*. Cool marshalling of evidence is not all there is to being human, and a good thing too! I think it is too hard on us to call us an *irrational* species. We are highly prone to neurosis and even psychosis, yes. We can be dangerously conformist, even when, as in our culture, the way that we conform is to claim that 'We are all individuals'. And we are only weakly moved by evidence alone. But that's because we are an *emotional* species. And emotion of the right kind and in its right place is not irrational. Passion, love, caring, joy, warmth, trust, even grief: these are what make civilised life worth living (and what make it possible in the first place). A cold, neutral, distanced, rationalistic attitude to everything embodies a profound failure to be mammalian, and to be human.

12. THE ROLE OF 'TEACHER' IN A DYING CIVILISATION

SA: You've just implied that you don't think that the answer we are looking for will come only or even mostly from universities. The popular conception of a scholar is that of a highly educated intellectual who is paid by society to educate the next generation. From this rather old-fashioned perspective, students presumably take university courses in order to be educated by experts about subjects of interest and importance. But when I stand before my students today, teaching my course 'Consumerism and the Growth Economy', I am uncomfortably aware that often, in matters of deep civilisational significance, I simply do not have a 'solution' to the crises we face; no clear answers to the questions I, or my students, pose about how to fix things. At most I can share reflections on better or worse responses to our global predicament. Or perhaps I should say global 'dilemma', since dilemma means we face a range of options that are all challenging or difficult; that there is no easy way out; perhaps no way out at all. How do you conceive of your role as a 'teacher' in a civilisation that is in decline?

RR: In answer, let me go back for a second to much earlier in the educational process. We are beings born in a state of extreme vulnerability and unformedness. When we are really young, there are some truths (such as mortality) that we need to be led into only slowly: to confront an infant mind with them immediately might break that mind, or break the spirit, break the heart. It's not right to translate one's spirit of honesty and truthfulness—a spirit that is foundational for everything I aspire to do and be—into a dogma of absolute frankness always about everything to everyone at all times.

But the terrible mistake that our civilisation has made, I believe, is to turn the truth about our dying civilisation into an excuse for lying systematically to our children. We lie to our children every time we pretend that they can expect an ordinary career of their choice in an endlessly growing economy. We lie to them every time we present them with an image of a 'typical' farm full of happy outdoor pigs, cows, and hens. We lie to them every time we tell them we love them while giving them a new piece of plastic crap before turning our attention swiftly back to our mobile phones. We lie to them, and ourselves, if we think or declare that we love them and yet the actions we take, rather than being directed with determination toward the aim of seeking to transform this civilisation for the better, actually hasten its likely collapse.

We lie to them because much of the time we lie to ourselves, of course. But also *because we are pierced by the thought that their innocence shouldn't be swept away instantly* before it has had any time to give them some feeling of safety within which they can become sanely 'attached' and sanely individuated. And, as I started by saying, there is a grain of rightness and truth in that approach.

But I think that we have got the balance badly wrong. There is no excuse for lying systematically, and with each year older a child gets, there is ever less of an excuse for not being truthful. By the time children have reached 18 or so, and maybe gone to university, there is absolutely no excuse.

It is abominable—although understandable, given peer-pressure and institutional pressures—that most academics are concealing from their students the dire realities and probabilities and possibilities that now hang over them. We ought to be frankly teaching our students at every opportunity about the extremity of the ecological crisis, about the out-datedness of their economics curriculum (and in fact, arguably, of most curricula), about how unmoored our species has become from reality. We ought to be teaching them, too, things like how to grow their own food, rather than pretending that they are all going to have 'wonderful' digital jobs and the like.

So that's my answer to your question. The first responsibility of intellectuals and of teachers at a time like this is to come clean. We should tell it like it is; and we should apologise for not having a better story to tell, a better world to bestow. We should be inspired by figures like Spartacus, Cato the Younger, Vaclav Havel, Mahatma Gandhi, Petra Kelly, Greta Thunberg: we should be clear that our power, such as it is, rests now in being authentic; in not shying away from extremely uncomfortable realities; in sharing how we feel. I find that one of the most powerful things I can do now is to share my fear (and grief) for the younger generation with them. That's the basis of real dialogue; real empathy.

We should be inspired by Wittgenstein, Socrates, Ivan Illich, and Paulo Freire in this way: we should be honest enough to admit that, as you say, Sam, we don't have the answers. What it is for us to teach includes the admission that we have no body of knowledge that, if picked up by the younger generation, would deliver a 'technical' (nor even any other kind of) fix. My generation has, on balance, failed in the epochal task of trying to wake this civilisation up before it sealed its own fate. Part of what we need to teach is *that*. And the humility that follows from that.

And here's the encouraging thing: My experience to date is that quite often, far from inducing a general depression, which is what we fear and compulsively try to avoid, the kind of honesty that you and I are mooting here, Sam, can be transformative. It is the basis for a radical new hope. Hope not founded on delusion or deceit. While giving frank talks about our existential predicament over the past few years, I've found that many people, especially perhaps younger people, have profound fear about the future of our living planet, fear that typically they have kept hidden, for fear of being ridiculed, or for fear of 'contaminating' others. When people are able to share their deepest fears then at last those fears may actually stop growing and gnawing. For now we can start to think together about what we actually *can* hope for, and how we may start to make it possible.

13. CRISIS AS OPPORTUNITY

SA: You alluded earlier to the saying that every crisis is an opportunity—from which the optimist infers that the more crises there are, the more opportunities there are! Of course, this statement must not be seen to be romanticising or desiring crisis like some dreamy-eyed fool. In fact, our entire dialogue seems to have been based on a deep pessimism about the prospects of smoother and less disruptive modes of societal transformation. So perhaps crisis might be our best hope for disrupting the status quo and initiating the transition to something else.

When the crises of capitalism deepen, as they seem destined to do in coming years and decades, the task will be to ensure that such destabilised conditions are used to advance progressive humanitarian and ecological ends rather than exploited to further entrench the austerity politics of neoliberalism. I recognise, of course, that the latter remains a real possibility, as did the arch-capitalist Milton Friedman, who expressed the point in these terms:

> Only a crisis—actual or perceived—produces real change. When that crisis occurs, the actions that are taken depend on the ideas that are lying around. That, I believe, is our basic function: to develop alternatives to existing policies, to keep them alive and available until the politically impossible becomes the politically inevitable.

It is not often that I am in agreement with Friedman. With reluctance I have come to the conclusion that it is probably only through deepening crisis that the comfortable global consumer class will become sufficiently perturbed that the sedative and depoliticising effects of affluence might be overcome. In fact, I feel it is better that citizens are *not* in fact protected from every crisis situation, given that the encounter with crisis can play an essential consciousness raising role, if it triggers a desire for and motivation toward learning about the structural underpinnings of the crisis situation itself.

RR: Yes, the danger, if we are protected from crisis for too long, is that we wait even longer than we would have done otherwise before addressing it. This is why Jared Diamond and others have emphasised the grave danger of highly unequal societies (such as, disastrously, the one we now inhabit): for the elite in such societies can fool themselves into thinking that things are basically OK way past the point of no return, while the masses suffer and start to experience collapse; and then it is surer that the society as a whole will collapse.

SA: And yet, as I have noted, crisis can go in many directions—it might be the wake-up call we need... or it might simply hasten the civilisational degeneration into barbarism. What role does crisis play in your views on transition? Is the world ready for the profound challenges that, in one form or another, lie ahead?

RR: We are now committed to climate disasters, and they will worsen, for a long time to come. But we do not yet know whether we are committed to climate catastrophe. It is just possible that the former may help enable us to avoid the latter. Consider the literature on 'Disaster Studies', in particular Rebecca Solnit's amazing book *A Paradise Built in Hell: The Extraordinary Communities that Arise in Disaster*. Solnit observes that disasters are often recalled by their survivors as periods of great joy and profoundly meaningful experience.

She argues that this is because, at these moments, the social order is revealed to be 'something akin to... artificial light: another kind of power that fails in disaster'. Its failure reveals a truer light, that comes from within us, that we can share and grow with one another. It unshackles moral resources which we had available to us all along— within ourselves, and in community waiting to spring into being— allowing 'a reversion to improvised, collaborative, cooperative and local society'. Moments of crisis allow us to see and to start to make, for the first time, a vision of a world we always sensed was possible, but had been unable to articulate, let alone to instantiate.

This is one vitally important way in which the long crisis we are entering into is without doubt an opportunity. The widespread assumption that disasters always unleash a cruelty or indifference endemic to human nature is false. This is the meaning of the title of Solnit's book: disasters often spontaneously produce not barbarity but generosity, community, something like a spontaneous non-dogmatic 'communism'.

The coming ecological and climate disasters could yet yield an improvement in human goodness. And even a consciousness—a determination—that we have to stop such disasters from multiplying into catastrophe. It is perhaps unlikely that this will come into being (enough); it is probably likelier that, instead, people's focus will too often stay narrowly present and local,[48] and that the bigger picture will be ignored or even denied. But the possibility of a new consciousness and conscientiousness is one of the few great hopes we have at present of civilisational transformation.

In any case, even if it turns out that the best that we can hope for is the second of the three 'options' with which I greeted your opening question to me—the option of seeding a successor-civilisation from the very-likely wreckage of this one—then it's still imperative to seek out the silver linings of disaster (and even of catastrophe). Learnings that will help us deeply adapt. Such as the way that the survivors of previous ecological collapses seem to have learnt humility with regard to nature. Our indigenous ancestors who decimated the world's megafauna in Europe, Asia, and Australasia, and who in many cases suffered dire consequences from doing so, learned better how to live in harmony with and in natural systems.[49] We *will* learn this lesson. The question is only whether we learn it as we die (1), or as we (or rather, probably, a few of us) survive collapse and start to construct a new way of living (2), or in order to transform ourselves and prevent collapse (3).

Similarly, we will go back to the land in pretty large numbers. The only live issue is whether we will do so in a part-planned and part-voluntary way sooner,[50] or in a catastrophically desperate, forced way later.

The crisis we face is above all an opportunity to learn, and to imagine and hope and *do* better. But some of that learning has to be pre-emptive. By the time collapse occurs, it may/would be too late.

SA: The prospect of societal collapse is gradually getting discussed more regularly these days, even in some mainstream forums, like prominent newspapers and 'serious' magazines. If it was once a fringe territory of 'doomsayers', today one might even say that collapse is the expected course of action. Slavoj Zizek would say this is functioning to 'normalise the apocalypse'. But for all the attention this notion of collapse is given, it is not always discussed with much rigour or definition. What do you mean when you use the term collapse? Is there any prospect of a 'prosperous descent'? Or will any collapse scenario necessarily be full of pain and suffering?

RR: This is a crucial question. The way I have been talking about 'this civilisation' (as finished) has been shorthand. What for? Basically, for what Joanna Macy calls 'industrial growth society'. *That* is what is finished. The fantasy of endless 'progress' (aka endless economic growth) is dead. Every further bit of material 'progress' now takes us further over the cliff-edge, reduces even further our slim chances of clawing our way to some safety. We are eating into our life-support systems.

Growthism, a central part of the ideology that rules this civilisation globally, is deadly because it always makes our task harder. You and I, Sam, are among those who have shown that net green economic growth while remaining within planetary boundaries is deeply implausible.[51] But *even if we were somehow wrong* about this, it would still be true that growthism tends toward deadliness; for, by making our collective aim into GDP growth, and thus by endlessly increasing pressure upon those boundaries, we provide a rod for our own backs.

Even if net (i.e., economy-wide, not sector-specific) green growth were possible, it's a rod for our collective backs. The intelligent thing to do, obviously, is to remove the rod!

As for industrialism, nearly everyone assumes that the industrial revolution was an inevitability and obviously a good thing. But this evinces a lack of imagination. As the consequences of industrial-growthism lead us steadily toward the white swan of climate catastrophe and ecological breakdown, with the sixth mass extinction well underway at our hands, surely we have to re-assess this assumption. Surely we have to take up a more critical and thoughtful stance toward it, as the Dark Mountain Project has helpfully done. Surely we have to ask: couldn't the whole thing have been done with more precaution, more slowly? And couldn't—mustn't—we be more selective about which industries we choose to permit and to develop now?

We need to rein in the reckless growth of industry, and to radically roll back the many industries that are killing us and our other-than-human kin, and steadily eliminating our kids' future. We need to *choose* which products and processes of industrial society we want to seek to preserve. For example, I hope that, in our radically relocalised future, we may be able to preserve some of the internet as a mode of communication, to help us share knowledge and wisdom, to continue to tackle global issues (such as climate), and to help prevent a growth in xenophobia. But we'll have to see. Without doubt, much of what we are accustomed to will have to go.

The sheer enormity and audacity of this task, and the way that it contradicts our ruling ideas of the allegedly endless technical ingenuity of humanity, the allegedly beneficent nature of technology, the ideology of 'progress' and 'development', etc., mean that it is hard to see how we could possibly do this. So what I am saying is: such a transformation, resulting in a society on a radically different footing, is not something that any wise person would *bet* on us succeeding in. A prosperous descent—which is path (3) of the possible paths that I laid out earlier—would be wonderful, and remains possible, and so it is painful (not to mention unbearably frustrating) to admit the fact that humanity appears very unlikely to be capable of it.

This is why, as I argued earlier, we need the insurance policy not only of transformative adaptation but also of deep adaptation; to help prevent path (2)—that of a successor-civilisation after a collapse-event—itself collapsing into being path 1 (total collapse; the default outcome, the white swan that probably awaits us, on even a reformed business-as-usual path). Some kind of collapse, quite likely driven by the interaction of water shortage and consequent food shortage, but quite possibly driven by other things instead or as well (e.g., by pollinator failure due to the insect-apocalypse, or possibly by plague among a climatically-weakened population), has to be considered our likely fate. Not just in Africa, Asia, and the Middle East, but in Australia, Europe, and North America.

Industrial-growth society is finished. We will rapidly transform it into something better, or it will collapse, either to seed something different or to simply end us. And any collapse event will be chock full of pain. It will be challenging to prevent it from becoming a more or less total collapse; for instance, as we have already discussed, stopping nuclear waste—spent fuel rods, not to mention live reactors—from becoming virtually endless drivers of death and suffering will require concerted effort at a time when we will be ill-placed to make that effort. (In countries like England or the USA, do we even have the collective will to make the sacrifices that may well be required under such circumstances? Is the combination of voluntary and forced heroism that prevented the disaster of Chernobyl from becoming a catastrophe replicable in countries like ours that pride themselves on an ideology of atomised individualism, countries which toy with the idea that there is no such thing as society?)

And yet, where the greatest danger lies, there too can be found the saving power. As we dare at last to gaze into the abyss, as we find the courage to contemplate these matters that you and I are discussing here, as we take the measure of the beauty of what we have and the folly of our squandering it, as we feel the heart-pain of what we are committing our children to, so we can rise to the challenge. Rise up to meet it. The greatest challenge of the entire history of our species is upon us. What an awesome and even thrilling responsibility—and, of course, terrifying.

As I set out in answer to your previous question, one thing that in this great and terrible moment gives me very real hope is that, when human beings are subject to the gravest of threats and the most unexpected of utter challenges, we really do tend spontaneously to become our best selves, selfless and creative of real community.

So it is possible that the disasters which are definitely coming and the collapse which they are likely to lead up to may yet be the making of us.

SA: You are suggesting then that even in a collapse scenario, we might be surprised to discover that some tragic events have a silver lining of sorts. Perhaps you could unpack that counter-intuitive idea a little further.

RR: Yes. We are living, nowadays, in ways that involve us in a virtually permanent absence of community. Disasters enable this to be overcome. They enable us in our small selves, our limited and limiting egos, to be overcome. For such overcomings to be possible and to take place, there must be a full-scale *disaster*, not merely an accident or something bad. Charles Fritz, who is a key influence on Rebecca Solnit's work in this area, emphasises this point.[52] He writes that disasters need to be big enough to *not* leave behind 'an undisturbed, intact social system'. Only if that system is disrupted sufficiently can new and realer forms of community emerge. 'Disaster provides an unstructured social situation that enables persons and groups to perceive the possibility of introducing desired innovations into the social system,' according to Fritz.

When we picture collapse, we tend to imagine human beings at their worst. But what is sometimes revealed in disaster is real community identity, which fulfils our modern lack; and this is the very opposite of what the Hobbesian 'script' would have us imagine.

The etymology of the word 'apocalypse' is uncover/reveal. I am suggesting that, while any collapse will necessarily involve much pain and indeed death, as we will no longer be able to support our artificially bloated population[53] and our decadent standard of living, it doesn't have to reveal a human nature that is red in tooth and fist. If we proceed from a place of love and fellowship rather than from a place of distrust, the *human nature that gets revealed even in collapse could be one of unexpected solidarity* and care and sacrifice.

Writers such as Margarete Buber-Neumann, Victor Frankl, and Primo Levi have made clear how, even in environments designed to break the human spirit, unexpected possibilities of loving-kindness often flowered. So it won't be beyond our wit (or our hearts), when under stress, to foster such flowerings in the years of living dangerously to come.

In collapse, our social system would of course get thoroughly—utterly—perturbed. What I am saying is that, in the less structured situation that emerges, there is a very real chance that we can find each other and find some deeper togetherness. So yes, this is a potential silver lining even of collapse, especially if we can turn a partial-collapse scenario into a breakthrough of the human spirit. A blitz spirit for our times. An arising of consciousness that could seed a successor-civilisation, a civilisation which someone like Gandhi would think a good idea.

In order to realise this possibility, we have to be willing to imagine far more boldly than is usual in the narrow confines of individualist neoliberalism, or even among 'progressives', 'leftists', or mainstream greens. As I've said, we can be inspired by the 'messages' of—and by the very success of—blockbuster films such as *Avatar, The Lord of the Rings, The Hunger Games,* and even of *The Road.*[54] Climate disasters or a collapse scenario will blast us out of what Charles Eisenstein calls our story of separation; we will be forced to quit the sad little silos that consumer culture encourages us to 'live' within. Amidst the trepidation, the fear, and (frankly) terror, as well as bitter prefigurative grief, that we rightly feel when we dare to contemplate courageously and open-eyed what the next 20 years or so of the human adventure will be like, we ought also to feel some new, radical hope: that the 'bad' times ahead will almost certainly reveal strengths and even joys that we didn't even know we were capable of.

14. STERILITY OF IMAGINATION

SA: You are asking us to imagine boldly. Consumerism, the ideology which possesses societies such as England or Australia today, seems to be based on an uninspired, narrowly materialistic conception of the good life, which strikes me as a gross failure of imagination and based on mistaken ideas of freedom and wealth. People might know, deep down, that something is very wrong with this cultural narrative—that there must be better, freer, more humane ways to live. But we live in a world that conspires to keep knowledge of such alternatives from us. We are told that consumerism is the peak of civilisation and that there are no alternatives, and over time, as these messages are endlessly repeated and normalised, our imaginations begin to contract and we lose the ability to envision different worlds, different ways of living and being.

Might today's crises be a function of imaginative sterility? If so, might the challenge of seeding a new civilisation be less about better evidence and arguments, and more about new *visions* of prosperity?

RR: To connect this question with one we tackled earlier: part of what we need is a vision of prosperity that is not a vision of 'growth'. Luckily, green economist Professor Tim Jackson has started to develop such a vision. His book is called, precisely, *Prosperity Without Growth*.

To fill out that vision a little more, I believe, as I implied already above, that it's crucial to emphasise the importance of *relocalising* our economy.[55] We need to imagine (and then bring about!) the *reversal* of much of the economic globalisation that we have suffered, a globalisation that has been the deliberate aim of global capital as expressed through the radical and awful 'trade' treaties that have come into play in the last generation.[56] We need to start to picture localities as becoming largely self-sufficient and self-governing again: we need in that sense truly to take back control.

Relocalisation will of course increase our resilience, by lessening our dependence on highly vulnerable long supply-lines and overly—absurdly—complex networks of economic dependence. We will provision ourselves mostly from our own bioregion.[57] This is especially crucial in terms of food provisioning (and here there are many signs of hope, from the growth in vegetable box schemes to the growth in community supported agriculture; from the growth in smallholding to the growth in permaculture and agro-forestry). But the moral applies generally across the economy.

Now, this is desirable in itself; it will free us from being dominated by distant corporations or markets (or governments); and it will make it less likely that we will despoil our ecosystems (because it is easier to trash a rainforest that is thousands of miles away than to trash one's own backyard, in the sense that one can see the effects immediately of the latter kind of trashing, and thus it's easier to be moved to stop). But there is a further reason why it is crucial at this moment in history: because we simply cannot rely on long supply-lines at a time of the potential collapse of the world food-system, and of world civilisation itself.

A different, less 'hungry' way of re-imagining ourselves[58] is not just a better way to live than consumerism on its own terms, nor even just a way of giving ourselves a shot at the unprecedented societal transformation we would need in order for this civilisation to survive, though it is very much both of those. It is also the beginnings of the mother of all insurance policies, which we now very badly need: a way of starting to construct a 'lifeboat' civilisation that can see humanity through the very hard times that are almost certainly coming, as a result of our ongoing savage and stupid destruction of the natural world.

Consumerism and economic globalisation are going to end. The only issue, once more, is: will we choose, intelligently, to end them voluntarily, or will a tortured and enraged nature force that ending upon us, in a violent collapse?

15. THE EXISTENTIAL VOID CONSUMERISM CANNOT FILL

SA: The assault that capitalism is making on the natural world is tragic and disgraceful enough. But it also seems as if the *culture* of capitalism strikes deeper still—to the core of our being, as we've already discussed. This isn't just about the despair that threatens to set upon us as we become ever-more aware that the global economy is destroying so much of our beautiful but fragile planet and threatening to bring an end to this civilisation. I am talking also about the failure of consumerism *on its own terms*.

Consumer culture seems to be spreading a sort of spiritual malaise, an apathetic sadness of the soul, as more and more people discover that material things cannot satisfy the human craving for meaning. Just look into the eyes of the person going to work on a Monday morning to live out their alienated existence under capitalism—people often seem to have faces subtly twisted with despair. Disconcertingly, we might see the flickering despair in our own eyes reflected in theirs. It also seems as if the abundance of stuff in consumer societies, as technology forecaster Paul Saffo argues, has merely produced new scarcities, creating an existential void that stuff simply cannot fill. We destroy the planet, and for what? For whom? To what end?

This might all sound very depressing, and it is. But hidden within this critique of consumerism is a source of hope. If it is the case that human beings just don't find mindless consumerism all that fulfilling, that seems to open up space for rethinking our relationship to material culture and actually living better while also consuming less.

The notions of moderation, sufficiency, and frugality have a long and venerable tradition in the history of philosophy. One thinks especially of the voices of Diogenes, Socrates, and the Stoics, to say nothing of the diverse range of spiritual traditions and indigenous cultures that warn against the dangers of materialism. It would seem that these diverse thinkers and traditions have something essential to teach us about how to manage today's (and tomorrow's) challenges.

RR: Of course! And yes, it is vitally important, and hopeful, that consumerism doesn't make us truly happy. If it did, then we'd *really* be in trouble! For then we'd be even harder pressed than we are to get collectively off the treadmill. But thankfully, people are gradually, painfully starting to realise that possessive individualism is a recipe for collective misery, to saying nothing of its also being a recipe for eco-catastrophe. If our culture really takes this truth in, it will change course.

And such a change of course will build (of course!) on the common-sense that says that what matters most to us is not stuff; it's family and friends, it's nature, it's peace, it's our values. We are divided between this commonsense on the one hand and the ideology of growth and of more, on the other.

As I've said, we are suffering in this way a crisis with a *spiritual* dimension. We're turning the planet—and the future—to junk, and not even making ourselves happy in the process. If we were to learn from the Stoics—or Jesus, or the Buddha, or Lao-Tze—we would understand this, and seek to live simpler, calmer lives, which would actually be highly likely to be happier.

For of course, nothing can *make* one happy. The pursuit of happiness is a dubious enterprise. Pursue love, pursue wisdom, pursue ground-edness, pursue the good for others—and happiness will take care of itself. But we get taught that everything can be bought, and that buying is everything. We get taught to *have* (or to *want*), not to *be*. And so, of course, we are too often miserable and bereft.

I'm reminded of a scene that a colleague of mine witnessed in a super-market, and which haunts me. A little kid is screaming at its mother, 'I want, I want, I want!' The mother answers, 'What is it you want? What do you want me to get you?' The kid replies, in an even more desperate scream, 'I don't know!' We try to fill the hole within us with things. But all that that does is feed a never-ending craving.

But I think it is really important not primarily to blame consumers for this. I argue that it is *producers*—and advertisers—who are primarily to blame. The concept of 'consumerism' is extremely useful for those who want to sell us things. Because it then seems as though they are only doing our bidding. *We* are the agents, seemingly: *they* are merely satis-fying *our* wants and needs. This is exactly how mainstream economics characterises the fundamental nature of human exchange: it's a matter of demand and supply. Supply exists, allegedly, only to satisfy demand.

I say that 'consumerism' is a piece of false consciousness, and in-deed a tool for our continued semi-enslavement (to our cravings).[59] The real push for us to be 'consumers' comes from producers (via marketers).[60] It is producers who need to sell us stuff, in order to extract a profit—and the most effective way that they can do so is to artificially create in us ever-growing 'needs'. That's where market-ing and advertising come in. Marketing/advertising are the selling arm of the producers' interests in our society. They are what turns us into consumers. Mainstream economics conceals this truth be-hind its rhetoric of individual consumers being the 'pull' factor at the root of economic exchange. But in fact, it is the 'push' factor that dominates—producers push their products at us continually, with thousands of coded messages a day. They even try to get us to blame ourselves for the disposal of the waste that such endless pushing inevitably creates: you wouldn't know from listening to gov-ernment and corporate rhetoric that by far the largest proportion of the 'waste' stream comes from corporations, not from households.

Our economy, our system, our world, is not really 'consumerist'. It is producerist. Capitalism is a producerist system. Its most brilliant product, its greatest achievement, its founding lie, is to produce individuals willing to participate in it, grateful for it, and ignorant of its real nature. Its ultimate product, that is to say, is consumers. It makes you and me into consumers. Producerism is a system—our system—the 'crowning glory' of which is to conceal from its workers and its bottom-level clients (those whom it changes in order to sell its products to them—i.e., us) its own real nature. Such that it becomes the accepted wisdom—and it even becomes a kind of pseudo-leftist or pseudo-ecological creed—that we live in a 'consumerist' society.

Producerism's subtlest product is consumerism itself. The production of consumers, of people as desiring-machines always wanting more, with inexhaustible 'needs', allegedly fuelling an endless need to expand the economy (and to eat up more and more of our ecosystems in the process: this is really what producerism is all about).

The producerist ideology has much responsibility for the situation we have been brought to. My approach is to be compassionate to 'consumers' (that is, citizens, people). So long as we think of ourselves as 'consumers' we are blaming the victim.

16. CULTURE AND POLITICAL ECONOMY

SA: This is getting into some really interesting and important terrain, both in terms of how current problems should be framed and understood, and how a transition to another society or system might emerge. Let's unpack some of the issues further. Permit me, if you will, a somewhat extended statement.

In 2006 I began writing my PhD on degrowth at Melbourne Law School, entitled 'Property beyond growth: Toward a politics of voluntary simplicity'. I was something of an oddball at law school, because I was reading radically counter-cultural sustainability literature—drawing on writings from Henry Thoreau to the Club of Rome—but analysing it through the structural lens of legal and political theory, including insights from Marx, as well as social movement theory.

I came to see that there were two broad schools of thought in relation to environmentalism, which we could call critics of 'consumerism' on the one hand, and critics of 'producerism' on the other. With respect to the former, there were those who thought that individuals in affluent nations were choosing to over-consume, thereby driving the environmental problems and taking so much for themselves that little was left for those in real need. From that perspective, coherent as far as it goes, it would seem the appropriate response would be for those who are over-consuming to consume less. This would reduce environmental impacts and leave more resources for those in destitution, and many in this broad school argued that reducing or greening consumption could often lead to increased wellbeing, too—so there was nothing to lose!

However, from a different perspective—the one you have begun to outline as 'producerism'—there was a growing recognition of the *systemic* dimension of the problems. Political economists would look at the 'sustainable consumption' or 'voluntary simplicity' literature and dismiss it as naïve, as failing to recognise that the problems are systemic and thus require a systemic response, not merely a lifestyle response. This critique was, and is, often quite devastating, especially to the early 'light green' environmentalists in the 60s and 70s, who thought we might be able to reduce or 'green' consumption within the existing system—turn the lights off, compost, and recycle—and thereby save the planet.

The essential insight of producerism, as you have neatly outlined, is that the root of the ecological crisis is in the systems of production, not so much in the cultures of consumption. After all, it is clear that our consumption practices always take place within structures of constraint, and those structures make some ways of living easy or necessary, and other ways of living difficult or impossible. Currently, the structures of growth capitalism make consumerism the default way of life for the majority of people in affluent societies. For example, it is very hard to escape driving (even if a person wants to) if the structure of their society does not have adequate public transport or safe bike lines, and if life has been designed such that it isn't feasible to get all one's needs met in a very local area. It is no good asking people to stop driving if driving is the only way they can get to work and feed themselves and their family. This type of example could be repeated endlessly, to highlight how, very often, it is hard to consume less in a society structured to maximise growth and consumption. The problem of consumer 'lock-in' is very real. So it is clear that looking at things purely from the consumption angle is deeply flawed.

But I feel there is something lacking in much of the literature on producerisim too, and I'd be keen to hear your thoughts on this. In my PhD—and in much of my work since—I set out to synthesise these two critical views, a project that is implicit in the subtitle of my doctoral thesis: 'toward a politics of voluntary simplicity'. My background in legal and political theory made me very cognisant of the structural problems highlighted by producerism; but my exposure to grassroots social movement theory and practice (including sustainable consumption perspectives) made me ask questions about *how structures change*. And here it is important to think through the relationship between culture (including cultures of consumption) and political economy (the capitalist system).

In considering this question of how systems change, one must acknowledge that we live in an age of almost despairing political paralysis, where governments seem to be locked into the growth model of progress. There is much governments could be doing to facilitate the transition to a post-growth society, but governments around the world seem unwilling or unable to transcend the economics of growth and its fossil energy foundations. So if we cannot rely on governments to lead, how will the system be changed? It is not enough to say the system needs changing.

While it is fashionable to dismiss personal, household, and community action—including reducing consumption—as politically ineffective and as being unable to deal with the systemic and structural nature of our crises, I contend that this dismissal fails to understand or explain how structures change. I recognise and accept the systemic nature of the crises facing our species but maintain that there will never be a politics or economics beyond growth until there is a culture that demands it, and culture is a product of innumerable actions and practices, large and small. There are structural constraints of course, but there nevertheless remains a realm of freedom within those (context-dependent) constraints where agency remains. To dismiss the household or community scale, therefore, is to dismiss the foundation of the polis.

Again, the political economists who highlight the systemic nature of the problems are quite right—the problems *are* systemic—but then does that make individuals and households powerless victims?

No, I do not believe that. *People* ultimately have the power, and the only way the system is to change is if people, acting amongst the grassroots, organise into social movements that change the system 'from below' through participatory democracy and collective action. Voting for candidates offering green change may be part of changing the system but only part of it. Waiting for governments would be like waiting for Godot—a tragi-comedy of two acts, in which nothing happens, twice, before the curtain closes.

My position, in short, is there will be no macroeconomics or politics beyond growth until there is a culture of sufficiency that demands it. We—ordinary people—need to prefigure one-planet living as far as we can, in our own lives and communities, seeking to establish highly localised economies based on sufficiency, solidarity, and moderation. This is not to say that the state or government has no role play in the transition that is needed; it is only to say that a post-growth or post-capitalist state will not be the prime *driver* of the new society, but instead be the *outcome* of social movements building new structures and cultures within the shell of the existing system, and eventually replacing that system.

This should not be conceived of as direct, consumption-based 'solutions' to the problems of over-production, but as necessary groundwork for creating the new culture of sufficiency that will need to precede any new politics or macroeconomics of sufficiency. For these reasons I do not privilege *either* a demand-side response (new cultures of consumption) *or* a supply-side response (new systems of production). We need both, but my view is that the former must driver the latter.

How do you see the relationship between culture and political economy? What role will ordinary people need to play driving the new world into existence through prefigurative action?

RR: I agree strongly with most of what you say here. The 'consumerist' analysis alone is hopeless: it *reflects* liberal individualist values in our society that de-politicise and make real change impossible. Because real change (as opposed to mere tinkering or nudging, which is patently utterly inadequate at this moment in history) is always *social* change; it always involves people understanding that they (we) can only change *together*, as part of a greater whole. The really dire thing about the 'green consumer'-led approach is that it involves a kind of systemic guilt-tripping that depoliticises. Sure, we should seek to avoid any unnecessary flying; but far more significant than our own choices as to whether or not to fly is getting something like a Frequent Flyer Levy instituted, nationally and internationally.

A decade ago, Sam, I might have pushed back against your claims that a macro-level 'producerist' analysis is not enough. But it has become clear that it is not enough, as we have drifted inertially into a situation where, as you say, it is unrealistic to plan on sufficient macro-level political-economy change on the kind of timescales we need. We can *hope* and even *aim* for such change, but to *bet* on it has now become unwise.

This is an underlying reason why what you've said has to be roughly right: we have to build seeds of a new system at community level within the shell of the old, because of the high probability that the old will fail at scale, perhaps catastrophically. We need, therefore, to have *good examples* that can be scaled up in that eventuality; and we need *islands of survivability* that can carry on if the collapse is rapid and near-total. This, as I see it, is the primary significance of 'Transition Towns', of most actually-existing permaculture and agro-ecology, and so forth.

Hopefully these kinds of things both model and drive the transformation of our society. They show what is possible; they inhabit it and show its desirability. For, in the meantime, they are pleasurable (recall the pleasures of easy access to tasty food satisfyingly grown or foraged by one's own hand), and they are ethical. But the dual purpose they serve is also to prepare us for the unprecedented storms that are almost certainly coming. They may provide seeds of a future civilisation that could survive and rise from the ashes of the collapsing hegemonic civilisation.

Meanwhile, it would be a strategic error to give up on politics and system-level action, as too many permaculturists and gardeners and even activists, not to mention 'doomers', are (perhaps understandably) tempted to do. What many in the Transition Towns movement have discovered, to their cost, is that much of what they want to change cannot be changed while political-economy systems are unchanged.[61] You cannot pre-figuratively re-centre local life onto walking, cycling, and horse-riding while elected politicians continue to worship the automobile. Your community supported agriculture may fail if it is undercut by cheap imports. And so forth.

We need vigorous, radical activity at *every* level: we need good people everywhere at this time to be sinking their savings into radical causes, standing for parliaments, putting their bodies on the line, getting involved in smallholdings and foraging, devising places to live that can be resilient in the event of social breakdown, looking at their careers and asking what better they could do in the time we may have remaining; and more. It would be a complete misreading of what I am saying when I say that this civilisation is finished to conclude that we should give up on electoral politics. But equally, it would be completely irresponsible, this late in the day, to *bet on* electoral politics or even politics of any kind being enough to see us through. That's why now we need Extinction Rebellion, *and* deep adaptation. (And it is crucial that XR calls for and seeks to start to initiate transformative and deep adaptation, rather than relying on demands for mitigation.) And in any case, as you say, Sam, electoral politics in a vacuum is apolitical. What chance we have of transformation of the right kind is definitely dependent upon a culture of radical community-level action, and of voluntary simplicity (which can liberate funds for the causes that need supporting, as we simplify and reduce our own individual and family needs).

We are called to rise up. That rising up needs to happen in our minds, in our hearts, in our local communities, and across our countries and continents. It needs and means cultural activity, intellectual change, political action, everything.

I would ask every reader who has made it this far to get serious about this. What are *you* going to do to manifest what is now called for? How can you pour your money, or your life (or both!), into shedding some light into the darkness of this time?[62]

17. THE BEGINNING IS NEAR

SA: We began this dialogue with you ruminating on the possibility—or probability—that 'this civilisation is finished', and we've now traversed expansive territories exploring some of the implications of that challenging thesis. As our conversation draws to an end, what closing words would you leave with our readers as they set out to digest some of the uncomfortable perspectives we've discussed? Can accepting that this civilisation is finished be a pathway toward empowerment rather than disempowerment?

RR: Ultimately, the acceptance that this civilisation is finished, while initially disorienting and certainly emotionally demanding, becomes liberating. This is what I've found; this is what many of those who have heard my talks in person or on video have realised, and they've shown me this, to my excitement and gratitude.

It is liberating, in that we are freed from the hopeless pretence that the show can be kept on the road. We are liberated from the nauseating lies of 'green growth', and from the stupefying discourse of 'sustainable development'. Understandably but harmfully, such fantasies have occupied far too much of the attention and activism of environmental NGOs and of most Green politicians for far too long. We can now let them go. We are free instead to seek to find a sacredness in life, to reach frankly for practices and attitudes that might be enough to redirect us away from the death-march we are currently on.

Furthermore, we are liberated from the assumption that life is about having a good time until one draws one's pension; for we can no longer assume that our civilisation will exist by the time we are old. We are freed from believing, without qualification, that we are obliged even to obey the law; for how could the laws of the land be binding upon us, given that they are committing us and our children to oblivion? Facing the reality of climatic-nemesis and of the sixth mass extinction, we will feel and face terror and grief and despair. But these do not need to trap us indefinitely. Instead, we can be dramatically freed and empowered.

SA: A last question. Who is this 'we' you keep invoking?

RR: I believe that *humanity* has a responsibility to put right what it's done wrong.

Now of course there should be unequal distribution of that responsibility. Those who inherit the benefits of past wrongdoings, for instance, should shoulder more of it. Where I write from, in Britain, we need to step up to the plate and acknowledge a greater share, because we benefited from having industrialised first. Furthermore, those who have what are essentially ill-gotten gains—e.g., those who have profited from burning fossil fuel in recent times, let alone those who have actively sought to lie about their responsibility for the resultant damage—bear much more responsibility still. Meanwhile, there are some who are clearly blamelessly stuck at the bottom of the heap in this failing-civilisation: a newborn child in a poor family, a mother starving in the Yemen.

But, while it is right to make such distinctions and to make them count, we also need to recognise that on balance we are in the future together, or not at all. Not even the super-rich will be able to survive what is coming, if what is coming is a global climatic or ecosystemic collapse. Sure, they may gain a few months, years, even decades. But in truth there are no winners in a future that looks like *The Road*. And in the end what survives of us are our values, and our children (and their children, and...). If we end the human adventure, if we end the bold experiment of civilisation, that ending will be as terminal for the rich as for the poor. The elite rich ought to realise this and pour their wealth now into creating a common future, not fantasise that their descendants will be able to make it through a world without bees and without ice.

So I honestly believe that in the end we really are all in this one together. Climate-criminals should be blamed, those who have contributed very little to the ecological crisis shouldn't; but in the end the blame-game doesn't take one very far. We'll survive and even possibly flourish by becoming better at building community, or we won't survive.

So in the end my use of 'we' aims to be very wide indeed. Of course, it is in the (very) end—and this is crucial—an *invitational* 'we'.[63] The point of this book, this conversation, is to invite the reader to *join* a project of saving our common future, to the greatest extent possible.

For while we are living in what some call 'Empire', it is a paper tiger. It has a sell-by date. Soon, as William Blake once prophetically put it, it will be the case that 'Empire is no more, and now the Lion and the Wolf shall cease'. Unless we manage to transform this civilisation, or at least to build lifeboats to take values worth preserving through the vast death throes of its collapse, then they probably won't. Instead, we'll be subject for a while, as part of a downward spiral, to new mini lions and wolves, new mini empires, of a very unpleasant kind: perhaps warlords, or the kinds of creatures that the majority of surviving human beings have become in the future as imagined in The Road.

We are on the road to some such future. But in such horrendous thoughts—in such realities—can be found, I have argued, our possible salvation. The stakes become clear. We are thoroughly liberated from domesticated hopes: of a normal career, of a secure old age, of ever-rising house prices. We are liberated from much peer pressure, from expectations of 'normalcy'. We are freed to engage in the kind of courageous way of life sketched and manifested by Extinction Rebellion. We are freed, by way of the place of honesty that you invited me into at the opening of this book, Sam, to contemplate the reality of incipient collapse and to prefigure what lies beyond it.

Your marvellous novel of ideas, Sam, *Entropia*, offers one vivid way of making a society aware of its need to become far more self-reliant and far less consumptive. Tragically, we do not have time now to undertake in the real world the scenario painted in your novel. But: we still have time to read it. And to engage in conversations such as this book has been. And that means that we still have time to relinquish, together, the unrealistic hopes that have pseudo-nourished us for far too long. We still have time to turn together to face reality. And to rise up to meet it.

As our earlier discussion relating to socialism implied, the old left vs. right division in politics is increasingly obsolete. The real divide now is between those—still the vast majority—who think that we can live on more than one planet and those of us who have accepted that our politics, in the broadest sense of that word, has to be based in place, ecological, terrestrial.[64] The crazed 'trans-humanists', who want to upload themselves into the cloud or to leave the Earth behind altogether in favour of colonising the stars, are actually *more honest* than the soft-denialist mainstream, which fantasises that we can live as if we had more than one planet while remaining humans tied umbilically to Mother Earth.

The real divide in politics now is between those who are willing to accept the end of growthism and to embrace instead a precautionary ethic as the new commonsense on the one hand, and those who favour recklessness on the other.[65] Believing that anything remotely like the status quo can continue *is* recklessness. The name of 'progress' may be used to seek to dignify it, but actually such a perspective is deeply backward-looking: to the fantastical era/error of industrial-growthism. An era, an error, that is finished, and that will finish us if we do not accept that profound fact; the profound change that we are called to witness and to co-create.

Once we accept that this civilisation is finished, we are free to seek a new beginning. To seek, that is, to co-create the next civilisation (whether or not we have to live through collapse in order to get there).

Better: the future is calling us to start to do so. The love and courage that we *are* demands nothing less. The alternative is too awful *not* to have the courage to contemplate it. We look an uncontrolled collapse—leading to warlordism, or indeed runaway global over-heat, maybe all the way to human extinction—in the eye.

And then *we do what it takes* to not let this be our fate.

POSTSCRIPTUM:
HELENA NORBERG-HODGE

I'm honoured to collaborate with Samuel and Rupert, both of whom are friends and people I greatly respect. They are among the rare academics who have the courage to go beyond the confines of narrow specialisation to speak out, to question the dominant narrative.

The crisis of our civilisation compels us all to search for root causes of our global problems, which in turn takes us beyond reductionism, beyond single issues, and calls into question what we really mean by 'progress'. On deeper inspection, we find that 'progress' is actually changes wrought by a global techno-economic system. A system which has come to threaten all life on earth. Where Samuel and Rupert use the term 'civilisation' in this context, I favour 'techno-economic system' because it helps us realise that the problem is not with human society itself, but rather with the inhuman system that has been imposed upon us. As we familiarise ourselves with the structures of this system—its drivers, mechanisms, and consequences—we become aware that it is a product of economic policy borne out of blindness and outdated colonial assumptions; it is neither inevitable nor unchangeable.

It's of vital importance to distinguish between two very different forms of progress. The past century has seen cultural trends that can generally be termed 'progressive'; we are moving away from the outright barbarism of the days of colonialism, and lessening the stronghold of white supremacy and patriarchy. The economic trajectory, however, has remained out of touch with those changing values, and has continued on a straight line from colonialism. Wealth inequality has expanded to record extremes, and slavery, cultural destruction, and domination over nature have only become more insidious. From its very inception in 17th-century Britain, the global economy set out to invade and undermine local economies, extract their wealth, and amalgamate them into a monocultural, centralised system. This was originally achieved through conquest, genocide, and slavery. In the modern era, with ever greater specialisation within large-scale technological systems, it has become increasingly difficult for individuals to recognise the overall impact of their actions. Whether worker, consumer, politician, or CEO, it's virtually impossible to be sure that you are not harming ecosystems or people on the other side of the world. It's as though our arms have grown so long we can't see what our hands are doing.

It is the global system that we need to examine more carefully in order to understand what has been happening to our societies over the last three or four decades. I want to add to the discussion about 'information deficit', to argue that a lack of information is in fact a major issue. We've been blind to the workings of the globalising economy, to the corporate overhaul of our society and all its institutions—the emergence of a de facto global government of corporations and banks. Big industry has managed to serve its growth prerogative by convincing national governments to ratify a series of trade treaties that have rolled out the red carpet for multinational business and finance, at the expense of people and local communities. The global players have been given the green light to scour the globe in search of the cheapest labour and laxest regulation, while local economies have been undermined, overregulated, and destabilised.

This has pulled people the world over into an accelerating rat-race, in which even the jobs of CEOs are threatened by megamergers. The production of virtually all our needs has been subjected to the profit-obsessed speculations of foreign investors and algorithms, gearing the entire world towards more energy- and resource-intensive, wasteful, mechanised mass-production and trade over vast distances. The absurdity of this system is perhaps most poignantly demonstrated by the phenomenon of redundant trade—countries are now routinely importing and exporting identical quantities of identical products. The UK, for example, imports hundreds of thousands of tons of milk, bread, and pork per year, while exporting hundreds of thousands of tons of milk, bread, and pork per year. Subsidies, taxes, and regulations—mechanisms that should be ours to use to shape the economy in whichever way we see fit—have been channelled into building up the infrastructure for resource-intensive, centralised economic control.

We have not been given this bigger-picture perspective. In its absence, we have been told that it's our fault that climate change is worsening; we are in denial, selfish, and unwilling to change. The corporate-controlled mass-media has distracted us with celebrity scandals and a schizophrenic theatre of left-right politics. Although this can all sound rather conspiratorial, as I alluded to before, it's my conviction that even CEOs and decision-makers are subjected to the same blindness that has kept us as citizens immobilised. They are caught up in bureaucracy, seeing the world through abstractions, trapped in a 'big is better', 'growth is good' narrative.

Although we regularly experience the consequences of systemic breakdown in our own lives, until recently, few have been connecting the dots between the issues we face on both personal and planetary levels and the economic juggernaut that has come to dominate the globe. We have not been told that the system driving climate change and species extinction is, in fact, the same system that is widening the gap between rich and poor, creating poverty and unemployment, and pushing each one of us to run harder and faster just to stay in place. This kind of blindness has served to keep us divided, self-blaming, bickering about single issues and absorbed in a politics of identity, while the underlying sickness of civilisation spreads.

The mass insecurity created as the drone-like global economy robs people of their livelihoods, identities, self-respect, and control over their own lives has left them forgotten, disillusioned, angry at the 'progressive', urban political establishment and inclined to vote for extreme right-wing parties. The spectre of fascist leadership in an increasing number of countries is arguably more frightening than the spectre of climate change, not least because it threatens to outlaw environmental protection and protest. For this reason, it is absolutely essential that we harness a systemic analysis to connect the economic and social issues faced by marginalised sectors of the population with our ecological predicament. I'm convinced we need a campaign that ties together our social and ecological crises and diagnoses their systemic root cause. We need what I call 'big picture activism' to build up enough political momentum to deal with climate change.

We must attempt to zoom out to see the system as a whole, place it in its historical context, and learn from more self-reliant, pre-colonial practices and worldviews. In doing so, we can call into question conventional assumptions about wealth and wellbeing, poverty, development and deprivation—are we really, as Bill Gates and Steven Pinker would have us believe, the most privileged generation ever to walk the face of the Earth? Can we even begin to imagine how much we have lost as we've been herded off the land into soulless high-rise buildings, cut off from community and from decision-making power? Broadening our perspective in this way sets us on track to expand perceptions of what is possible and desirable for the future of our species, beyond the Western-centric, urban-centric vision of a techno-utopia that Silicon Valley's billionaires would have us believe in.

It is true that we can go no further with this civilisation—we need fundamental systems change. It is equally true that this is almost entirely good news! The growth prerogative of this inhuman system is leading to ever greater social fragmentation, imprisoning people in cutthroat competition, joblessness, ruthless individualism, and spiralling epidemics of addiction and mental illness. A fundamental shift in direction, therefore, is not only a prerequisite for preventing further damage, but is also an immense opportunity for deep and widespread healing.

As we remove our dependence on the centralised, corporate-run economy, we inevitably begin to reweave the fabric of local, human-scale interdependence. We start to build localised economic structures, which reconnect us with each other and with the earth, creating the structural basis for community and for our own psychological and spiritual wellbeing. The localisation of economies moves us away from homogeneity and nourishes the diversity of ecosystems, cultures, and individuals that makes up the richness of life on Earth, and slows us down to a pace at which we can more genuinely appreciate the uniqueness of every being.

At the grassroots around the world, the seeds of a worldwide localisation movement are already germinating. In a common-sense way, people are responding to various forms of breakdown, and coming together to regenerate place-based relationships, economies, and cultures in a myriad of creative ways. From community gardens to farmers markets, from alternative learning spaces to local business alliances and co-ops, countless initiatives are demonstrating the deep healing that springs from turning away from the consumer culture and reconnecting at the local level. I have seen prisoners transformed, delinquent teenagers given meaning and purpose, depression healed, and social, ethnic, and intergenerational rifts bridged.

The shortening of distances between the production and consumption of our basic needs is the most effective way to immediately reduce CO_2 emissions. It also leads to another fundamental shift; because local markets demand diversity (rather than huge quantities of standardised commodities), production is encouraged to shift away from machine-run monocultures to favour diversification and more jobs for people. It has given me great joy and hope to see a kind of 'agriwilding'—the rapid recovery of both agricultural and wild biodiversity on previously damaged land—and to see the simultaneous creation of meaningful, community-based jobs on that land.

Given the huge systemic supports for the big and the global, from lavish government subsidies and tax breaks to corporate-owned media and heavy biases in funding for academia, the continued flourishing of these alternatives is a testimony to the power of community—to the motivation, perseverance, and strength that emerges when people come together to create positive change. They represent a fundamental departure from the colonialist dreams of industrial capitalism, and put forward a very different vision of the future—one in which human beings find their way home to community and to Mother Nature.

Increasing numbers of people around the world are beginning to wake up; they see cracks in the consumer-capitalist façade, failures in our so-called 'democracies'. What we need now is a meaningful explanation of what has gone wrong—a structural diagnosis—and a vision for the future that can motivate people from all walks of life to challenge the status quo. The articulation of this vision must therefore not limit itself to the ecological arena—it can and must include powerful arguments about the economic and psychological benefits of transforming civilisation as we know it, and thereby get far greater numbers of people on-side.

We are facing collapse on multiple levels, but the good news is that the crises we face are interconnected—they share a root cause, and there is a systemic strategy for beginning to solve them simultaneously. This book is an example of the kind of 'big picture activism' we need in order to get people to zoom out, see their commonalities with unlikely allies, and unite voices for a fundamental shift in direction. We have the opportunity to create a people's movement; a coalition like never before. I agree with Rupert and Samuel that the end of civilisation as we know it gives us an opportunity to create the conditions for both human and ecological wellbeing.

Endnotes

1   See R. Read. 2017. 'This civilisation is finished...'. *Green Talk* (8 June 2017). Available at: http://greentalk.org.uk/wp/this-civilisation-is-finished/ (accessed 25 March 2019).

2   See R. Read. 2018. 'Climate change: Once we no longer deny it, then we might just have the will to try drastically to change course'. *TLE* (14 March 2018). Available at: https://www.thelondoneconomic.com/opinion/climate-change-once-we-no-longer-deny-it-then-we-just-might-have-the-will-to-try-drastically-to-change-course/14/03/ (accessed 25 March 2019).

3   This thought is partly anticipated in Roy Scranton's important book, *Learning to die in the Anthropocene* (2016).

4   What would (2) or (3) look like in detail? I'll offer partial examples as this conversation continues, but let me mention immediately that there is a key role here for *fiction*. Starhawk's *The Fifth Sacred Thing* or Samuel Alexander's own *Entropia* are very good stabs at (2). Ursula le Guin's anarchist 'thrutopia' in *The Dispossessed* is possibly the best realistic vision we have of (3) (but it has no specific bearing on our climate and ecological predicament). There is far more work here for artists to do. See also, R. Read. 2017. 'Thrutopia: Why neither dystopias nor utopias are enough to get us through the climate crisis, and how a "thrutopia" could be'. *Huffpost* (6 November 2017). Available at: https://www.huffingtonpost.co.uk/rupert-read/thrutopia-why-nei-ther-dys_b_18372090.html (accessed 27 March 2019).

5   See, e.g., J. Bendell. 2018. 'Deep adaptation: A map for navigating climate tragedy' (IFLAS Occasional Paper 2, 27 July 2018). Available at: https://www.lifeworth.com/deepadaptation.pdf (accessed 25 March 2019). See also some of the work by John Foster, Jonathan Gosling, and the 'Dark Mountain' move-ment. I do not include here the now-well-known work of David Wallace-Wells because, although this work is very useful, it does not face up properly to the tripartite dilemma that I have just set out. Wallace-Wells remains unwilling to consider possibility (2), and does not consider possibility (3) adequately. Instead, he is in the end strangely optimistic about the prospects of keeping some majorly-reformed version of our current civilisation on the road. He seems to be psychologically compelled to this as an alternative to the only other scenario he sees: the Earth becoming uninhabitable (i.e., my (1)). He appears unwilling to take seriously the fragilising effects upon our prospects of sheer human numbers, and his having become a father seems more or less by his own admission to have clouded the clarity of his vision of our likely future prospects. For my response to Jem Bendell, see R. Read. 2018. 'After the

IPCC report, #climatereality'. *Medium* (15 October 2018). Available at: https://medium.com/@rupertread_80924/after-the-ipcc-report-climatereality-5b3e-2ae43697 (accessed 25 March 2019). See also, Read, R. 2018. 'Post-civilisation' (IFLAS Occasional Paper 3). Available at: http://iflas.blogspot.com/2018/12/post-civilisation-iflas-occasional.html (accessed 25 March 2019).

6 Though not nothing. If we went extinct, for instance, it would be infinitely worse if we took down bonobos, elephants, wolves, and the social cetaceans with us than if we didn't.

7 It is just-about conceivable that this civilisation might survive by adopting an extremely disciplined eco-fascism. See R. Read. 2018. 'Post-civilisation' (IFLAS Occasional Paper 3) for some discussion. Available at: http://iflas.blogspot.com/2018/12/post-civilisation-iflas-occasional.html (accessed 25 March 2019). This might seem to violate my claim that this civilisation is finished. But I am not convinced that it really does; such a way of life, literally requiring some kind of fascism, should, I think, not properly be regarded as *civilised*.

8 See N. Taleb, R. Read, R. Douady, J. Norman, Y. Bar-Yam. 2014. 'The precautionary principle with respect to genetic modification of organisms' (NYU School of Engineering Working Paper). Available at: https://arxiv.org/pdf/1410.5787.pdf (accessed 25 March 2019). We've argued the same vis-à-vis climate change: See N. Taleb, R. Read, J. Norman, Y. Bar-Yam. 2015. *Issues in Science and Technology* (Summer 2015). Available at: https://necsi.edu/climate-models-and-precautionary-measures (accessed 25 March 2019).

9 See for instance D. Spratt and I. Dunlop. 2017. 'What lies beneath: The scientific understatement of climate risks'. Melbourne: Breakthrough Institute. Available at: https://docs.wixstatic.com/ugd/148cb0_aod7c18a1bf64e-698a9c8c8f18a42889.pdf (accessed 25 March 2019). Of course, this does not imply that the precautionary principle is now irrelevant to climate. See, e.g., R. Read. 2018. 'APPG Briefings on the Precautionary Principles'. Available at: https://agroecology-appg.org/ourwork/appg-briefings-on-the-precautionary-principle-climate-change-and-animal-welfare/ (accessed 25 March 2019). See also, N. Taleb, R. Read, J. Norman, Y. Bar-Yam. 2015. *Issues in Science and Technology* (Summer 2015). Available at: https://necsi.edu/climate-models-and-precautionary-measures (accessed 25 March 2019).

10 D. Fischer. 2014. 'Climate risks as conclusive as link between smoking and lung cancer'. *Scientific American*. Available at: https://www.scientificamerican.com/article/climate-risks-as-conclusive-as-link-between-smoking-and-lung-cancer/ (accessed 25 March 2019).

11 We need to remember that any uncertainty is a two-edged sword—things could end up *better or worse* than expected. It is profoundly reckless to assume, as 'climate-sceptics' do, that current climate science is 'alarmist'. It is worth noting the deeply-worrying fact that the actual changes in our climate over the last two decades (and especially just in the last few years) have been consistently worse than median climatological predictions, and in some cases have been worse than the supposed worst-case scenarios.

12 See D. Nuccitelli. 2014. 'The climate change uncertainty monster—more uncertainty means more urgency to tackle global warming'. *The Guardian* (4 April 2014). Available at: https://www.theguardian.com/environment/climate-consensus-97-per-cent/2014/apr/04/climate-change-uncertainty-stronger-tackling-case?CMP=Share_iOSApp_Other (accessed 25 March 2019).

13 D. Spratt and I. Dunlop. 2017. 'What lies beneath: The scientific understatement of climate risks'. Melbourne: Breakthrough Institute. Available at: https://docs.wixstatic.com/ugd/148cb0_a0d7c18a1bf64e698a9c-8c8f18a42889.pdf (accessed 25 March 2019).

14 For detail on what is meant here by 'catastrophe' see John Foster (ed.). 2019. *Facing up to climate reality: Honesty, disaster, and hope*. London: Green House. This book, authored by the Green House collective, is constructed around the difference between disaster (inevitable) and a collapse-inducing catastrophe (still just avoidable).

15 See R. Read and N. Taleb. 'Religion, Heuristics, and Intergenerational Risk Management'. *Econ Journal Watch* 11(2) 219–226. Available at: https://econjwatch.org/articles/religion-heuristics-and-intergenerational-risk-management (accessed 25 March 2019). Arguably, the closest we have actually come to imagining the world with only people in it is to be found in Cormac McCarthy's *The Road* (and in the film thereof): hardly a hopeful example. I discuss such extreme anthropocentrism in Ch. 3 of R. Read. 2019. *A film-philosophy of ecology and enlightenment*. London: Routledge.

16 This is exactly what some are doing. See, e.g., M. Lynas. 2011. *The God species: Saving the planet in the age of humans*. Washington: National Geographic.

17 A critical reader might ask: But do you practise what you preach? Isn't this conversation full of prognostications that exceed the evidence? The answer is: No, it's not. I make one large semi-substantive claim: that this civilisation is finished. Because the only way it will now appear to survive is if it morphs into something very different. Beyond that, I mostly offer warnings, scenarios, ideas, adding up to a precautionary ethic and politics that would protect us in case of collapse and would give us a shot at transformation. I don't practise futurology here.

18 Some readers may be nervous about the way I am using the word 'nature' here. To dispel those worries, please see R. Read. 2013. 'Nature in the "anthropocene" age? Mediating between Monbiot and Poole'. *Talking Philosophy* (23 July 2013). Available at: https://blog.talkingphilosophy.com/?p=7380 (accessed 25 March 2019).

19 The question of exactly which technologies should survive the breach that is coming is beyond the scope of this book. That question is in part itself a technical question; it is also in part a question that should, as I am arguing, by subject to democratic will and thus cannot be *settled* (though it can be *informed*) by philosophical considerations (see my essay co-authored with Helena Paul on this in John Foster (ed.). 2019. *Facing up to climate reality: Honesty, disaster, and hope*.

London: Green House). It is in part a question that will be settled willy-nilly by accidents of future-history and path-dependency. Briefly, it is I hope clear that, as Heidegger helped us to see, there are important distinctions to be made between technologies that do not work against the grain of nature and technologies which seek to dominate nature: consider the difference between a watermill and a high dam that creates a lake in its wake.

One fascinating and important specific version of this question is whether the internet should survive. My hope is for a future in which we are able to retain information-technology and long-distance communications, so as to co-ordinate with regard to global environmental threats, and so as to guard cosmopolitanly against the danger that a newly relocalised world might retreat into a xenophobic parochialism. But we need also to frankly acknowledge not only the massive ecological and carbon damage caused by the internet and by computing more generally, but also the serious cultural damage they cause through homogeneity, the chronic way that they distract people from nature (from reality!), their actualised potential (whether through Facebook or through the kinds of *Black Mirror* things being done by the Chinese Government) for anti-democracy and indeed for totalitarianism, and more besides. At some point, there should be a serious debate about the future existence of the internet.

One thing that is for sure is that assessments of the viability for humanity of technologies needs to be truly long-termist. Nuclear power would not even be considered by a society that was appropriately long-termist. (See, on this point, the important film *Into Eternity*, which sets out the intractable dilemmas of very-long-term management of nuclear waste, etc.) The only reason that it is being considered by a few greens is the desperateness of our short-term plight. This brings out a difficult irony of our situation: our paradox being that, while we desperately need to build a culture of long-termism, we are in a situation where we need urgent action: i.e., where everything drives us towards short-termism!

20 For those not yet convinced, see D. Ehrenfeld. 1978. *The arrogance of humanism*. Oxford: Oxford University Press.

21 K. Anderson. 2015. 'The duality of climate science'. *Nature Geoscience* 8: 898–900.

22 E.O. Wilson has created a vision of how it could be done across half the planet, in his book *Half-Earth*. If we hadn't been so determined that the present book be short, we would have spent more time discussing the biodiversity crisis and its existential implications not only, obviously, for the creatures we are extinguishing but also, potentially, for ourselves, with pollinators the most obvious case-in-point. Our primary focus upon the climate crisis risks marginalising the biodiversity crisis (and other desperately pressing crises, such as the soil-depletion crisis). This risks perpetuating an insufficiently ecocentric perspective. One excuse for this focus is that it remains the best way of really getting the attention of human beings. But that says something less-than-ideal about humanity.

23 See N. Taleb, R. Read, R. Douady, J. Norman, Y. Bar-Yam. 2014. 'The precautionary principle with respect to genetic modification of organisms' (NYU School of Engineering Working Paper). Available at: https://arxiv.org/pdf/1410.5787.pdf (accessed 25 March 2019).

24 R. Meyer. 2018. 'What happens if we start geo-engineering—and then suddenly stop?' *The Atlantic* (25 January 2018). Available at: https://www.theatlantic.com/science/archive/2018/01/what-happens-if-we-start-geo-engineeringand-then-suddenly-stop/551354/ (accessed 25 March 2018).

25 Precautionary reasoning is under constant attack from those who wish to profiteer from the dropping of precautionary constraints on their action. This campaign of attack is somewhat ironic, given the fact that the groundbreaking and exhaustive research of the 'Late lessons from Early Warnings' (European Environmental Agency, 2013) programme of research showed that the reality is that the Precautionary Principle has only relatively rarely been actually used. Usually it has been deployed too late, if at all (and sometimes when it *has* been deployed it has been deployed ineffectually). Moreover, it is, of course, a fallacy to reason from the fact that we have survived thus far to the conclusion that we must have been precautious enough. We have in fact had several very narrow escapes (and probably more that we don't know about). For example, as Paul Crutzen has pointed out (in his Nobel Prize acceptance speech), it was mere happenstance that chlorine-based compounds rather than bromine-based compounds came to be used in fridges. *If bromine had been used, then the ozone layer would probably have been almost completely destroyed, thus ending civilisation as we know it, before scientists had even realised what was going on.* This is a chastening example of our failure to act precautiously not destroying us—merely because we were lucky.

What would acting precautiously have meant in relation, say, to use of new chemicals in fridges and voiding them into the atmosphere? It would have meant, for instance, proceeding slowly with them, allowing them to be used experimentally (including initially in controlled sterile environments) *before* rolling them out en masse. Such a change would be, frankly, enormous: it would have considerable impact on the 'speed of life' and the pace of economic change and economic growth. But that 'cost' cannot be weighed in the balance against the immeasurably greater cost that is incurred by a human race that destroys its own conditions of habitability—as is currently happening.

26 Though the change that took place last year has been a harbinger of a process of ongoing improvement in this regard at the BBC. See, e.g., T. Payne. 2018. 'One of the most pressing issues of our time'. *Radio Times*. Available at: https://www.radiotimes.com/news/tv/2019-03-06/bbc-natural-history-environment/ (accessed 25 March 2019).

27 It would be unwise to infer from this that everything GDP leaves out should be monetised, for that would make the mistake of assuming that there is no harm done when anything and everything is 'internalised' to the economy. But there is much harm done, not least through the further potential self-aggrandisement

of economists. That is why I have resisted the imperium of the discourses of 'ecosystem services' and 'natural capital'. See R. Read and M.S. Cato. 2014. 'A price for everything? The "natural capital controversy"'. *Journal of Human Rights and the Environment* (Sept. 2014): 153–167.

28 This is the key reason why Jeremy Rifkin's recent ideas—ideas that have attracted many adherents in our society, which still yearns for a techno-fix— for a new wonderful techno-utopia are a dangerous fantasy.

29 See R. Read. 2016. 'Precaution vs. Promethean: The philosophical dividing line that will define 21st century politics'. *Rupert Read*. Available at: https://rupertread.net/precautionary-principle/precaution-vs-promethean-philo-sophical-dividing-line-will-define-21st (accessed 25 March 2019).

30 See G. Kallis. 2017. 'Radical dematerialization and degrowth'. *Philosophical Transactions of the Royal Society A* 375 (20160383): 1–13.

31 See P. Victor. 2019 (2nd edn). *Managing without growth: Slower by design not disaster.* Cheltenham: Edward Elgar; T. Jackson. 2009. *Prosperity without growth: Economics for a finite planet.* London: Earthscan. What Jackson and Victor are showing is that the idea of 'green growth' is incompatible with not breaching planetary limits.

32 Why the scare-quotes? I am nervous of the term 'degrowth', partly because it risks conjuring an image of a future which is qualitatively continuous with the present, and only qualitatively different. But that can't be right. A society that is genuinely transformed will involve different ways of life from ours. It will not merely be a shrunken version of what we already have. Socialism went wrong because it absorbed seamlessly the materialist accumulative/'producerist' emphasis of capitalism. We need a shift to a different dimension.

33 This is an ugly word, but I make no apology for using it—for 'growthism' is an ugly thing.

34 *Obviously* I don't agree with his methods; I have always been a practitioner of strict non-violence, most recently in Extinction Rebellion.

35 To understand why it is not, consider that the most ambitious proposals that exist for a renewables-powered zero-carbon Britain, those of the Centre for Alternative Technology, imagine this happening by 2030. That is an eye-watering target, and time is running out for it. If we are to reach zero-carbon by 2025, we will simply have to cease large chunks of harmful economic activity.

36 The UN has at last implicitly recognised this, in its most recent report, on the locked-in warming of the Arctic: see https://www.theguardian.com/environment/2019/mar/13/arctic-temperature-rises-must-be-urgently-tack-led-warns-un (accessed 27 March 2019). The deadly feedbacks brewing in the Arctic make clear that the alarming, unprecedented 1.5 degree report in autumn 2018 was still too *optimistic*; for that report, unacceptably, basically ignored such feedbacks.

37 See R. Read. 2018. 'Religion after the death of God? The rise of pantheism and the return to the source'. *Medium* (19 January 2018). Available at:

https://medium.com/@GreenRupertRead/religion-after-the-death-of-god-the-rise-of-pantheism-and-the-return-to-the-source-54453788bbaa (accessed 25 March 2019).

38 See, e.g., J. Studley. 2018. *Indigenous sacred natural sites and spiritual governance: The legal case for juristic personhood.* London: Routledge.

39 Moreover, spiritual practice does not have to be non-secular. On this point, see the argument in S. Batchelor. 1998. *Buddhism without beliefs: A contemporary guide to awakening.* New York: Riverhead Books. See also the practice of much contemporary Quakerism.

40 Obviously, this is very different from the attitude I criticised earlier as our tacitly 'worshipping' ourselves. We need to have faith in ourselves that we can learn from our (dire) mistakes, as many indigenous peoples did, and that we can change. Whereas the attitude of self-worship foolishly tends toward glorifying us *whatever* we do, sometimes by way of saying that what(-ever) we do is in our nature (as if that settled anything about what we should do or be), sometimes by way of claiming that we have somehow 'transcended' nature—when it is increasingly obvious that we haven't.

41 Which is not the same thing as saying that *romanticism* should be avoided. I don't believe it should be. A sure sign of the decay of our culture into a managerialist technocracy is the hegemonic assumption that romanticism is *prima facie* an error; my view, following Iain McGilchrist's analysis in *The master and his emissary* (2009), is instead that romanticism at its best (for instance as found in Wordsworth and Coleridge's *Lyrical Ballads*) is actually a vital element of what should survive in our culture, and that romanticism can help us to transcend industrialism.

42 It should be noted that the current mental health crisis, while all-too-real, will be over-shadowed by the *coming* mental health crisis: when most of humanity wakes up to civilisational decline resulting from ecological devastation, then, as I imply at the end of this book, unprecedented epidemics of anxiety, depression, and despair will break out. But that coming pandemic might yet be the making of us, if we listen to it, work through it, and change our common future to make human and non-human life safer again. In other words: the growing mental health pandemic is, if seen in the right light, potentially a good thing. It evinces a growing inner conflicted-ness, which we might yet choose to resolve by choosing life and connection, rather than the material culture of death.

43 This does not, of course, license a *longing* for apocalypse. The risks and downsides are far too extreme for that. Instead, we need to take the harder path of keeping the thin hope of transformation alive. I explain in detail why it is that longing for catastrophe is psychologically easier than seeking to act courageously when realistic grounds for hope are absent, in my *A film-philosophy of ecology and enlightenment* (Routledge, 2019), especially in Ch. 6.

44 In this way there is a crucial difference between science and technology. Pure science can largely be left to go its own way, and discover truths; not so, technology. Tragically, our time has forsaken the pure impetus of

scientific inquiry for the power and control that high technology promises. This point helps explain how we can be as dangerously immune to scientific evidence as we generally are: consider, for instance, the hostile response to Rachel Carson's disclosures in *Silent Spring*.

45   R. Read. 2013. 'Avatar: A transformed cinema; a transformation of self (and a transformation of the world'. *Film Thinking Collective*. Available at: http://thinkingfilmcollective.blogspot.com/2013/10/avatar-transformed-cinema.html (accessed 25 March 2019).

46   See H. Service and I. Zohar. 2010. 'Report: China bans *Avatar* from 1,600 cinemas due to fear of popular revolt'. Haaretz (20 January 2010). Available at: https://www.haaretz.com/1.5049164 (accessed 25 March 2019).

47   I'm thinking here, for example, of the work of George Lakoff.

48   A worrying fictive depiction of this possibility is to be found in John Lanchester's thought-provoking new climate-dystopian novel *The Wall* (2019).

49   I am drawing here on the argument of T. Flannery. 1994. *The future eaters: An ecological history of the Australasian lands and people*. New York: Grove Press.

50   The process should begin by making it easier for those who wish to work on the land to do so: e.g., by tilting the food system radically in favour of community supported agriculture, smallholdings, etc., and by legislating major land reform.

51   See generally, Samuel Alexander's work (available at: http://samuelalexander.info) and R. Read. 2014. 'Post-growth common sense: Political communications for the future'. *Green House*. Available at: https://www.greenhousethinktank.org/uploads/4/8/3/2/48324387/post_growth_commonsense_inside.pdf (accessed 25 March 2019).

52   See C. Fritz. 1996. *Disasters and mental health: Therapeutic principles drawn from Disaster Studies*. University of Delaware Disaster Research Centre.

53   How should our population be reduced so as to return to something within Earth's carrying capacity? This demands a book in itself. I hope we can all agree that it should start with voluntary non-reproduction: educating women, choosing to have fewer or no children, going on 'birth strike'. And it is important to reduce the human population in *rich* countries too—because we are the ones who are plainly over-consuming.

54   My readings of these films can be found in R. Read. 2019. *A film-philosophy of ecology and enlightenment*. London: Routledge.

55   For detail, see H. Norberg-Hodge and R. Read. 2016. 'Post-growth localisation' (Local Futures and Green House). Available at: https://www.greenhousethinktank.org/uploads/4/8/3/2/48324387/post-growth-localisation_pamphlet.pdf (accessed 25 March 2019).

56   Do I mean here to include the EU itself? I am not going to get into that vexed question here. The interested reader can consult the articles I co-wrote with Helena Norberg-Hodge on this. See, e.g., H. Norberg-Hodge and R. Read. 2016. 'We must localise the EU and curb corporate power—but does that

mean in or out?' *The Ecologist* (31 May 2016). Available at: https://theecologist.org/2016/may/31/we-must-localise-eu-and-curb-corporate-power-does-mean-or-out (accessed 25 March 2019).

57   On how this will work, see, e.g., M.S. Cato. 2013. *The bioregional economy: Land, liberty, and the pursuit of happiness*. London: Earthscan.

58   See S. Earle. 2017. 'Imaginaries and social change'. *Medium* (1 February 2017). Available at: https://medium.com/@samraearle/imaginaries-and-social-change-2e0c8c093c25 (accessed 25 March 2019).

59   I say *semi*-enslavement because, while we are under assault from advertisers, especially now with the new tools in and of social media, that assault never totally succeeds. We retain our agency. The approach Sam and I pursue aims to *increase* that agency. At the same time, it must be conceded that the prognosis isn't wonderful; the world's masses seem pretty deeply *hooked* on consumerism, even though it doesn't make humans happy. Even now, it's mainstream 'commonsense' that we need more things and more flights etc., forever. The 'right' to fly etc. is widely taken as a given, and action to deal with ecological crises has to work around that. Unless and until that attitude changes, then humanity is heading directly for a dire collapse.

60   On the way in which 'marketing' is itself a deceitful term, see R. Read. 2009. 'What is "marketing"?'. *Green Words Workshop* (7 October 2009). Available at: http://gww.rupertread.org/what-is-marketing/#more-54 (accessed 25 March 2019).

61   See my dialogue with Transition Towns founder Rob Hopkins on this point: R. Read. 2008. '"Transition Towns" are great—but they won't save us, without help'. Available at: http://rupertread.org/transition-towns-are-great-but-they/ (accessed 25 March 2019); and R. Read. 2008. 'A point by point response to Rob Hopkins'. Available at: http://rupertread.org/point-by-point-response-to-rob-hopkins/ (accessed 25 March 2019).

62   For full-scale development of this crucial point about your agency, reader, in response to what you are reading here, please watch https://www.youtube.com/watch?v=4NT8EY73LCg (accessed 27 March 2019).

63   And the implication of this is that sometimes we just don't know who our 'we' encompasses, just how far it reaches. I invite you to join those of good faith who are striving together to do nothing less than change the course of history. Increasingly, we are legion.

64   My discussion here is influenced by B. Latour. 2018. *Down to Earth: Politics in the new climatic regime*. Cambridge: Polity Press.

65   See R. Read. 2016. 'Precaution vs. Promethean: The philosophical dividing line that will define 21st century politics'. *Rupert Read*. Available at: https://rupertread.net/precautionary-principle/precaution-vs-promethean-philosophical-dividing-line-will-define-21st (accessed 25 March 2019).

Rupert Read works closely with environmental scientists, in ecological philosophy, at the University of East Anglia. His publications include a number of academic and popular books, including *Philosophy for Life: Applying Philosophy in Politics and Culture* (2007). He blogs on environmental reframing at Green Words website and has two chapters in the new Green House think-tank book: *Facing up to Climate Reality* (2019). Rupert has written for *The Guardian*, *The Independent*, *The Ecologist* and many other popular newspapers, magazines and websites. He was a Green Party councillor in Norwich from 2004–2011. In June 2018, he triggered a BBC policy shift by publicly refusing to debate a climate change denier, which ended the presenting of climate change deniers' views as a counterbalance to scientific standpoints. His recent talk titled 'Shed A Light: Rupert Read—This civilisation is finished: so what is to be done?', presented at Churchill College Cambridge, is gaining viral impact on YouTube, having been viewed over 70,000 times.

Samuel Alexander is a lecturer and researcher at the University of Melbourne, Australia, teaching a course called 'Consumerism and the Growth Economy: Critical Interdisciplinary Perspectives' as part of the Master of Environment. He is also a Research Fellow at the Melbourne Sustainable Society Institute and co-director of the Simplicity Institute. Alexander's interdisciplinary research focuses on degrowth, permaculture, voluntary simplicity, 'grassroots' theories of transition, and the relationship between culture and political economy. His current research is exploring the nexus between degrowth and urban studies. He is author of thirteen books, including *Degrowth in the Suburbs: A Radical Urban Imaginary* (2019, co-authored with Brendan Gleeson); *Carbon Civilisation and the Energy Descent Future* (2018, co-authored with Josh Floyd); *Art Against Empire: Toward an Aesthetics of Degrowth* (2017); *Just Enough is Plenty: Thoreau's Alternative Economics* (2016); *Deface the Currency: The Lost Dialogues of Diogenes* (2016); *Prosperous Descent: Crisis as Opportunity in an Age of Limits* (2015); *Sufficiency Economy: Enough, for Everyone, Forever* (2015); and *Entropia: Life Beyond Industrial Civilisation* (2013)

CPSIA information can be obtained
at www.ICGtesting.com
Printed in the USA
LVHW011947131221
706074LV00013B/2147